Kiss Your Money Hello!

(AND FINANCIAL STRESS GOODBYE)

BILL HINES, AFC®, ADVISOR/PLANNER, EMANCIPARE

WILD LAKE PRESS, INC

To my lovely wife Lori, whose bright and inquisitive mind has driven much of my learning on these topics.

To my mother Carol, whose love and encouragement guided me toward the first college degree in our family history.

To my children and grandchildren—a code you can live by.

To every honest, hard-working one of you beautiful readers who yearns to breathe financially free.

"When we strive to become better than we are, everything around us becomes better too."
Paulo Coelho

"The more you learn, the more you earn."
Warren Buffett

"I say always follow your passion, no matter what, because even if it's not the same financial success, it'll lead you to the money that'll make you the happiest."
Ellen DeGeneres

"The successful warrior is the average man, with laser-like focus."

Bruce Lee

"The secret of getting ahead is getting started. The secret to getting started is breaking your complex overwhelming tasks into small manageable tasks and then starting on the first one."
Mark Twain

"If you don't know where you're going, you might end up someplace else."
Yogi Berra

Contents

Introduction

WELL, HELLO THERE!

Why this book? Right now, you may be browsing a few personal finance books in a library, bookstore, or even online. Why this one? Is it worth a couple of dollars and hours of your time?

Here's why. I've read the others. Almost every book was by someone telling their own personal rags to riches tale. That's admirable and impressive, but the likelihood that it's even close to you and your personal situation is quite remote. What worked for them will probably not work for you. Everyone is different, every situation is unique. Some assume their readers all want to be mega-rich. In my experience, most people just want to be happy, without money stress, and have a good, fun, comfortable life. It's much easier once you lower the bar! That said, if you want to be rich, I'll show you how to do that too. So many people reach that first goal, but add to their stress by constantly wanting more, never being satisfied. Trust me, no matter how much money you have, someone else is going to have more.

So (get to the point, Bill!), why this one? Because *this* book is based on my experience as a financial counselor, investment advisor, and financial planner. ***This is a user manual for your money!*** No matter who you are, there is plenty for you. There's stuff for broke folks to wealthy folks. This book takes you from zero money to money hero. We cover the Financial Independence/Retire Early (FIRE) movement as well. Young people are wising up about corporate tactics that pit them in a hunger games style survival competition against their friends in the adjoining cubicles. They're fighting back with tactics like quiet quitting and FIRE. Capitalism is all wonderful and fun until someone loses a tooth. Free yourself!

This book is the way to financial peace, to relieving the number one stressor in our otherwise beautiful lives and relationships. Most relationships end because of money. Most crimes are committed because of money. This book is the guide to living every day on your own terms, and never having to go to a job you no longer love, of never having to miss those important life events because, *work*. Despite my reputation as a notorious sender of TL;DR (too long; didn't read) emails, I'm going to keep this short and simple—just the way your personal finances should be! The first word of the title is no coincidence, by the way. KISS also means Keep It Simple Silly! Maybe I'll even make you laugh once or twice. Your household is a mini-business, only you measure success in 'happy', not some corporate financial metric. Each one of these chapters could be a book of its own. My goal is to keep it to just the essential content.

I'm not going to guilt-trip you about buying a latte. I'm going to convince you that doing the right things ***now***, getting over the hump in a short period, means buying all the lattes and new cars you want, with cash, not credit, for the rest of your life. Those lattes will taste *so* much better, and you'll enjoy the ride more in a car you own, not the bank. You'll watch the former car payment money grow like weeds in your investment accounts.

Can you trust me? Yes, you can. This book's for you. My favorite rock musician, Neil Young, once wrote a song called This Note's for You. It was a message to his fans that he wouldn't create music for big, greedy corporations or allow his music to be used in their commercials. His music is for the people. That's how I feel. That's why this book costs less than the others. I've done well by learning and living through the lessons in these pages. I've helped countless people do so, and I want you to do well. I want you to be happy, and enjoy this one life we get (as far as we know!). **This book isn't just for you—this is generational knowledge for your kids and parents.** Even if you're young, read the chapters on Social Security, Medicare, investing, and retirement planning and share them with your parents. Are they making expensive mistakes? They'll thank you. You owe them. Show them they may actually retire now! It might keep them from having to move into your basement someday.

Who am I? When I was a kid, I was a huge superhero fan. I'd sit in the corner luncheonette and read comic books on my way home from school until the owner would throw me out. I didn't have the money to buy them, my parents didn't have the money to give me. Peeking out from my bedroom at night, I'd see my mother stressing out over a kitchen table full of bills, writing out checks and stuffing them in envelopes. *Kiss your money goodbye*, I heard my father often mutter (hence, my title for this book!). He came home from work exhausted, especially as he got older. I naively begged him to retire—I didn't find out until he passed away that he had no means to do so. I didn't want to be the superhero who could fly, be invisible, shoot lasers out of my eyes, or swing from building to building on spider webs. I wanted to be the kind that could help people like my parents. That's where the title of this book came from. Instead of paying your hard earned money out to everyone under the sun, watching each paycheck or retirement distribution fly away, you're going to welcome it back, and kiss it hello. *Hi there, hard earned money! Let's have some fun together!*

I want to do that for you. Warren Buffett (one of my financial heroes) said, "If you get to my age in life and nobody thinks well of you, I don't care how big your bank account is. Your life is a disaster." That's my goal, too. Mr. Buffett, besides being arguably the greatest financial mind in like, ever, drives used cars and lives in the same house he bought in 1958 for $31,000. That's interesting, but the goal of this book is not to get you to pass up the things you want and love in *your* life. It's showing you how to get them. The goal is not money or wealth, the goal is happiness. For example, I'm now wealthy by the standard of my parents, but certainly not on that of someone like Buffett or Gates. I don't aspire to that. I'm happy. It sickens me to see billionaires so greedy that it just isn't ever enough. They have to keep right on screwing people over.

I became that superhero, and I believe I still am. I started a company called Money Coach Group (moneycoachgroup.com) and helped *so* many people get on their feet. You'll read about some of them in these pages. That company is now under new management with a like-minded new owner! As I did that work, I found that as the people got to positive cash flow and looked for investment advisors to help them build wealth; they were being rejected for not having half a million dollars, or being accepted and then being subjected to egregious fees or sold horrible insurance products. It really upset me, so I got registered as an investment advisor and financial planner and started Emancipare (emancipa re.com), which I run to this day.

Most of the personal finance books I've read should be titled, *I Will Teach You to Make **Me** Rich.* That's not a dig at Ramit Sethi. He seems like a great guy and wrote an influential book that's helped countless people, the same way I want to. His book talks about imagining your Rich Life. My book is about happiness. Most people would rather be happy than rich. Money doesn't solve all problems, but it sure solves a lot of them. Let's eliminate one of the biggest obstacles to happiness in most people's lives—money stress. That said, most of the personal finance gurus load their blog posts, social media posts, and books with things like affiliate links that line their own pockets. Or, their free content and books are simply lead-ins to get you to buy the big-ticket items they push, like expensive classes. I won't do that (other than offering inexpensive one-on-one personal help for those that need and want it). ***This book is for you.***

This is ridiculous, Bill! We have no extra money! We live in a van down by the river! That skit was funny on Saturday Night Live, but poverty is no joke. I've helped clients who came to me with no savings and negative cash flow or no job. Our first steps will be to show you how to increase your income and save money on almost everything. Those two steps, along with monitoring your cash flow, are a big part of changing your life and moving to-ward building wealth. We'll start with a basic, simple plan and then present options to tack on that are well-suited to your interests and passions, be they hustling credit card points/miles, building an investment property income, or just taking delight in using every personal finance hack in the book (this book!).

What about YOLO? To that, I say, "Exactly." You only get one life. Why spend it stressing about money, slowly but surely digging yourself deeper into a hole? Let's find ways to make money, instead of (or maybe while!) sitting around in your free time watching other people do things. Then, maybe you can actually go to those events, prime seating, living in the moment's electricity, instead of your recliner. Maybe following your favorite teams or artist around the country in an RV, seeing and living in its beauty. Living life. Real YOLO.

One more thing about this book. I'm going to resist the temptation and clutter of trying to do screen shots for some tools I discuss. The problem is that they're typically outdated as soon as they're printed. Same with hyperlinks—they often move. I'll keep this book as clean as possible for you, and provide the base domain names and short URLs so you can get to the places I'm talking about with the least hassle possible.

Need more help? We do mentoring, private and employee classes, investment advising, and financial/retirement/FIRE planning at emancipare.com. If you're digging out of debt, our friends at moneycoachgroup.com have inexpensive, one-on-one coaching to get you where you want to be quick. However, I truly believe everything you need to know is in these very inexpensive pages.

Let's get this party started!

CHAPTER ONE

Simple Days, Simple Ways

TAKE IT EASY

"Too many people spend money they earned..to buy things they don't want..to impress people that they don't like."

Will Rogers

L ife sure was simple back in the olden days, just a few generations ago. There were no credit cards, no credit scores. People went to work, got a paycheck, and each month that money went into the bank. Then they used a checkbook or paper and pencil to add it up and pay the bills, being careful not to spend more than they had earned that month. They put the extra money in savings. Monthly expenses comprised a few items; food, rent/mortgage, utilities, clothing, medical, gas and service for the car. No debt except the mortgage. You didn't buy things until you had saved up for them. Everyone had pensions. There were no 401ks and so forth. You worked until age 65, and then took your pension and social security and enjoyed your golden years. Grandma wasn't twerking on TikTok and grandpa wasn't stepping out on Tinder.

Think about that. Sounds kind of nice, doesn't it (not the oldies twerking and on Tinder)? You really didn't even need that paper and pencil after a while—your monthly income and expenses (cash flow) were so simple you could keep them in your head. Wow! Compare that to today. We're coerced, normalized, and brain-washed into a life where most monthly expenses would take pages to list. We carve each precious, hard-earned paycheck into pieces and scatter it to the winds electronically.

When you pay expenses with credit cards, the nice, clear monthly cash flow is now cloudy and obfuscated. If you buy those $200 kicks today, did you spend the money this month or when the credit card bill comes due a few months from now? Dunno. That's the point. If we're kept in a state of confusion, doing things be-cause we perceive "everyone else is" and "that's the way it is now," we yield our happiness, and we invite financial stress. We submit ourselves to the giant machine that profits from these mistakes, and sacrifice our enjoyment of this one grand life we're given. The machine of soulless corporations doesn't want you to see clearly that you're spending more than you're making. Why? It's bad for profits. They want us all to be a part of a soylent green, plugged-in matrix of cash flow into their already bulging coffers. Worst of all, we hurt our beloved children by behaving badly with money. They see everything. They feel the stress. Is the instant gratification of being able to so easily buy things before you have the money worth all that?

It doesn't have to be that way. Imagine you and your partner made your debt (other than the mortgage) disappear. Poof! Now you're back in those olden times (careful, the whole TikTok/Tinder thing is still a thing though...). Now, instead of spending countless dollars each month on interest in car payments, student loans, personal loans, and credit cards, you have actual money to save and invest. You're building wealth and are likely already financially independent. That's "take this job and shove it" kinda money. As JL Collins says in his wonderful book *The Simple Path to Wealth*, that's F-You Money. What's left to argue about? You guys want a boat or RV? Now you have extra money each month to save until you can pay cash. That means you get a *massive* discount on those big-ticket items. It means you actually own them, instead of fake-owning them. They're so much more enjoyable, especially since you won't have to work late into your 60s and beg your boss for time off to enjoy them!

That's what this book is all about. How to eliminate your debt quickly and strategically, and build wealth. How to save money on everything you purchase. Finding the perfect, fun side hustle that will probably turn into a lucrative small business (because, like, you actually enjoy doing it). Hacking your financial life in every department imaginable. Winning. Smiling.

How can you tell that you're doing it right? If something is simple and understandable, you're likely doing it right. We have this illusion that winning with money has to be complicated. We're bombarded with messaging about complex financial products or services. People in the business lead you to believe they have some secret sauce to get you to the top quickly. Crypto. Gold. Real estate. Options. Alternatives. Indexed or variable annuities. The old, misleading "we do better when you do better" or "we'll help you find a trusted advisor" pitch. The list goes on and on.

The biggest dirty secret of personal finance (we'll cover lots of them in this book) is that simpler is better. If something is complex or unclear, run. It means you're going to help someone else build wealth and become financially independent, not yourself. Nobody beats simple. We'll go into detail on that in the chapters on investing as well. It's not that hard. It's so easy, you can do it yourself. The goal of this book is to show you how. The goal of this book is to take you from:

Normal: Paycheck carved up into tiny pieces scattered to the wind as soon as it hits your bank account, hundreds to thousands in interest payments each month

to

Unicorn: Simple, clear cash flow, zero to low interest payments, consistent investments, working toward clearly outlined goals, no money stress, family small business, financial independence.

Before we start for real, here's a pep talk. Like anyone else that's about to embark on a big journey, such as quitting drinking, smoking, gambling, it may intimidate you. The voices in your head or from your friends and family may already cause you doubt. Some people get intimidated or jealous when they see a person trying to do something big. The friends at the bar will just laugh at you when you come in and say you're going to quit drinking, right? Tune it all out. Don't even debate or talk about it. Set an example. When they see you living your new life, they'll come around with questions.

In the beginning, you're standing at the foot of a mountain, looking up. That sucks. But if you can just take those first steps, something magical happens. Now, you can look back at how far you've come. And the journey ahead is shorter. You're closer. As well, the intensity is up to you. Keep going, as long as you're making progress. Give yourself grace for any setbacks—you're only human. Just keep going, no matter what. I've often seen clients start out somewhat timidly with the techniques we'll discuss. Then, they gain confidence and build up steam. They become gazelle-intense, as Dave Ramsey says. Their snowball of progress crests the hill, then picks up steam and size as it rolls effortlessly downhill. Like any other bad habit or addiction, this may take a few attempts. I highly recommend the old "just do it" approach. It's life-changing stuff. If you have kids, they're watching.

I said not to debate this with folks, but let any very close family members or friends know that you're going to be behaving differently, so they don't think you've joined a cult. Tell them you're going to be putting yourself first for a while, so that you can help them later. Put your oxygen mask on first. Teenage kids are tough. They live in a very status-oriented and judgemental tribe of peers. Sit them down and talk to them like adults. Tell them you're changing your life because you're currently setting an example that could ruin theirs. Remind them you're doing this so you can leave them something wonderful behind when you pass. Tell them you're doing this so that when they get that first job, spouse, and house, you aren't moving into *their* basement for the rest of your life. Ask them to imagine having to change both the baby's diapers and yours. That usually gets them.

Let's talk about credit scores for a moment. It's mostly over-hyped BS by the debt industry to get you to borrow more, keep you on that hamster wheel, chasing the score. Borrow more, more, more! Bull. It also doesn't affect your auto insurance rates. It's useful if you're getting ready to rent or buy a home, but there are ways around that, such as manual underwriting. Don't fall for the credit score repair/boost schemes. (Experian Boost isn't bad though, based on reports.) If you follow the advice in this book, your credit score will miraculously improve. Don't fall for the scams that claim they'll make your consumer or IRS debt go away, either. There's no magic other than following the guidance in these pages and doing the work.

<checks watch> Ok, let's close out this chapter with a few important bullet lists, gained from our years of experience with countless folks just like you. Real stuff!

The three most common problems that cause financial stress are :

- **Not enough income.** Sometimes people were doing just fine, carving up that paycheck pizza, living the dream. But then, someone got disabled in an accident, developed a long-term illness, got laid off and could not find work, or died. Life comes at you fast. We can fix this with our chapter on the many ways to build your income and build up an emergency fund.

- **Living above your means.** Lifestyle creep, YOLO, keeping up with the Joneses has an enormous price to pay. Many of those folks "doing well" with the big cars and homes have been my clients. Behind those gilded doors, they're unhappy, stressed, and fighting. They're drowning. We'll talk about how to get rid of expensive homes and cars. It ain't easy, but it can be done. Lose those boat anchors (and the whole boat, RV, or whatever is shackling you).

- **Lack of visibility/control.** As I mentioned earlier, most folks just do not know whether they're spending more than they're making. Debt and buying things before you have the money can create this problem. Do you have clear goals for all the milestones throughout the rest of your life (kids' college, vacation/2nd home, next cars, weddings, long-term care) and currently a plan and contributions toward them? Can you state your monthly income, expenses, and positive/negative cash flow? Your average monthly grocery and restaurant expense? When it's simple, you'll be able to do all that.

A few prerequisites and priorities:

- **Use a good bank.** You shouldn't be paying fees, ever, for anything. I'm a big fan of credit unions—you're a part owner, and they treat customers well. Read Google and Yelp reviews to find a good one. If you're a vet or military, Navy Federal Credit Union always scores well, if you have one near you. Online banks like Ally are amazing, but you can't easily deposit cash if you ever have to do that. If your regular bank/credit union doesn't have a high-yield savings account with the ability to create virtual savings buckets (we'll get into this later) start one at Ally.com. Don't pay annual fees! I don't care how good the bank (or credit card!) is. Don't be a fool by paying them for the privilege of holding your money (and profiting from it). Does anyone still use Wells Fargo? I know I personally never would, after what I've seen them do to their customers (and my clients).

- **Save up at least $1,000.** We'll show you how to get it done quickly and legally in the next few chapters. Put it in a savings account that's connected to your checking account (same bank/credit union) and make sure there's an automatic overdraft transfer feature set up (with no fees!) This prevents you from running back to the teat of credit cards or loans the first time something unexpected happens.

Finally, here are the keys to financial bliss. We're going to teach you about all of them, and take you back to a simpler, less stressful time.

- **Simplify.** When your financial life is simple, it's easier to manage and track. It's waaay less expensive and less stressful! It allows you to maintain control, especially as you get older and cognitive abilities decrease.

- **Emergency Fund.** This keeps you from running to the credit cards or personal loans the minute Murphy (the bringer of bad karma) shows up. It's an actual 0% loan that's not an expensive gimmick!

- **Paying Attention.** An effortless way to see your cash flow and whether you're on track for all those exciting goals ahead.

- **No Debt.** Except your mortgage, and then only for a short while. No interest cost—that moolah is all regularly invested and growing like weeds.

- **No layers, no lock-ups.** *The fewer people and rules between you and your money, the better.* (Except, not under your mattress or buried in the backyard!) Get expertise/guidance when you need it, but this isn't that hard.

Most people have a rat's nest of accounts going on. How do you manage something like that mess? You don't. It's stressful. Simplify that. Have one checking account with an overdraft savings account attached to it. You should have one IRA each. Roll any old employer 401k/403b/457b/TSP accounts into that IRA and close them. You should each have one Roth IRA and a joint brokerage account plus one shared in-case-of-emergency-break-glass credit card. Plus, your retirement plan at your current employer, and a HSA if they offer it. Simpler, right?

OK, are you ready? I am!

Chapter Two

Go With the Flow

Knowing Where Your Money is Going

"You must gain control over your money or the lack of it will forever control you."

Dave Ramsey

I won't give you some spiel about how you must neurotically track every penny you spend. Who wants to do that? Well, some people do. This book is about happiness, not drudgery. However, you need some way to know whether you're going in the right direction. You wouldn't head off into the woods at night without a flashlight and expect to get to your destination. The goal is to know your monthly cash flow, even if just at a high level. The good news is that there are many ways to do that. We just have to find the one that best suits you. No matter which one you pick, it should take no more time each day than making a cup of coffee or brushing your teeth. That's not too big a price for that someday vacation home, or walking into work each day knowing you don't have to be there if things go south.

Here's the basic concept, in a nutshell. Grab a paper and pencil, or other note-taking app or method that works well for you.

1. Add up the money you expect to come into your bank account next month.

2. List your expected expenses/payments for next month (use last month's statements if needed). It's OK to spitball at this point. Don't forget unusual events like birthdays.

3. Subtract the expenses/payments from the expected income.

That's your expected cash flow for next month. If it's negative, we'll fix that. See those lines where you listed your expected expenses and payments for next month? Hey! That's your budget for the month! Fooled ya! Congrats and great job. What's left to do? Suppose you put down $800 for groceries. When the month starts, the first time you go to the grocery store, get a receipt. That's your reminder. Put it somewhere you'll see it at the end of the night, like a pocket, purse, or your phone case.

Remember how we talked about this taking only a few minutes a day, like when you make coffee or brush your teeth at the end of the night? During one of those ritual times, just pull out your receipts for the day and update your budget. If you spent $125 on groceries, cross that $800 out and put $675. That's your remaining grocery budget for the month. Do that for any receipts from the day (or previous day, if this is your morning habit).

The magic in this is that within a month or two, you know exactly what your monthly expenses are. That's a big deal in financial success. It's a key to the solution you've been dreaming about. If you find you'll be over-running your grocery budget, you'll see other categories where you might be under-spending, and borrow from them (interest free, again!)

After the next few chapters, you should have some pretty good positive cash flow. Suppose we get you to a good starting point, such as $500/month extra, after you pay the bills. We want to draw that line in the sand. You can put it in the budget as an extra payment on a high-interest credit card, or your car payment, to make those disappear out of your life more quickly. Imagine how much easier it is to keep your monthly expenses in your head when you can count them using just your fingers! That's what happens when the debt payments are gone and it's just the basic stuff.

In fact, there's the lazy person's method of tracking cash flow, where you don't keep track during the month. If you feel you'll have $500 extra at the end of the next month, just schedule that extra payment for then. If it doesn't work out, and the money's not there around the 25th or so, just lower the extra payment or cancel it. Obviously, this isn't good, so at that point you should circle back and figure out where you overspent. If you don't trust yourself, or really want to play hardball with yourself, you can make that extra payment at the beginning of the month. That's drawing a line in the sand! It might make for some hungry days toward the end of the month, though. You'll look back on them fondly and tell the grandkids stories about it when they come to visit you at the family beach house legacy retreat you've purchased along the way.

I've shown how you can do this old-school with pencil and paper. If you're a spreadsheet nerd, there are plenty of free budgeting spreadsheets out there (vertex42.com), or you can easily make one yourself. There are great apps that are free or low-cost, such as Mint, Simplifi, EveryDollar, YNAB, and Quicken. I listed those from simplest and least effort to more effort/features. They do a great job of auto-categorizing your purchase, e.g. McDonald's is restaurant/dining. All you need to do is break down purchases at places like Costco or Walmart into the proper categories. That's not a lot of work! Put your products into groups at checkout to make it easier. Hey, notice how I didn't put in a bunch of sleazy affiliate links to enrich myself or have you question my bias or recommendations. This book is for you.

Ok. There's one more catch. Got a spouse/partner/significant other? This is teamwork. Most times, one half of the relationship deal is more motivated and engaged than the other. That's OK. But both halves must be in the loop. You're a team. Even if that means just showing the other person the budget you came up with. If they're sharing in the expenses, they have to know what the monthly targets are and where you stand throughout the month. This is important, because if one of you is standing in front of a nice pair of shoes for sale, the money has to be in the budget before pulling the trigger.

How to do that? For paper and pencil, use a small pocket-sized notebook and each person goes out the door in the morning with the current available spending in each category. If it's a spreadsheet, use Google Sheets, which is cloud-based, and hence always available on your phone. If it's an app, they all have varying ways of accomplishing that. Another key concept here is to just focus on one month at a time. It's an easily digestible, bite-sized chunk of time to monitor cash flow.

Another old-school approach is the envelope method. For example, on the first of the month, you take out the $800 for groceries and put it in an envelope. When you head to the store, you grab some, and just return the change to the grocery envelope when you get home. It's a bit messy and risky, but works for some people.

Credit Cards

Cash flow becomes pretty easy if you just use cash and your debit card, just like the simple old times we all yearn for, and as discussed in Chapter 1. The minute you put things on the credit card, it all goes to hell. If you buy that $200 coat on October 14 with a credit card, did you spend the money in October, or in December when the credit card statement and bill show up? It obfuscates this clear view of your monthly personal finances! I could make a case for just paying the card off by the end of the month.

But, I've seen plenty of folks that chased those points and miles by putting everything on their cards, thinking they were outsmarting the banks by paying it off each month. Guess what happened to those folks with huge monthly credit card statements when Covid-19 hit and they both lost their income, even temporarily? Right, the credit card companies know eventually, something will happen. Then they move in for the kill with ridiculously high fees and interest rates, and your financial life spirals out of control. Don't forget—often there's an extra fee for using a credit card, because merchants have to pay those fees. Pay attention and ask if you aren't sure.

You might ask, "Do **you** have a credit card, Bill?" In full honesty and disclosure, yes I do. Just one, a 2% cash back card I've had for ages. It's there behind the glass in a case that says, "Break in case of emergency." For example, once our debit card got hacked, and we had to wait a few days for a replacement. In that interim, we used the credit card when necessary. We recently went on vacation, and since we always have a zero balance on the credit card, we used it during our trip for vacation expenses, which allowed us to contain them, and then when we got home just transferred the balance from our vacation savings fund and paid it off.

If we're going to make a very large purchase, such as an appliance, we'll use the card to get the cash back and extra warranty protection, then pay it off immediately. That happens rarely! That is the extent of our credit card usage. There's hardly ever anything on it. We never pay interest or fees, and it's always paid at the end of the month to contain expenses in the same month. By the way, when the debit card was hacked for a small amount, our bank removed the bogus charge right away. With today's technology, banks pick up fraud almost immediately, so it's not like someone is going to run around Europe blowing your cash. Your debit card likely has a Visa or Mastercard logo on it, and if you call customer service and ask, you may find you have the same protections as your credit card.

Cash Flow Example

I don't do a lot of images in this book, but this one is essential. Check the Sankey flow diagram below. This is how simple your monthly cash flow can be once you get rid of all the expensive garbage, like credit card and car payments. Notice that money used for sinking fund/bucket savings each month for vacations, holidays, and car repair/next cars! Notice the nice chunk going to savings/brokerage every month. This is a simple example, adjust as necessary. This is what success looks like!

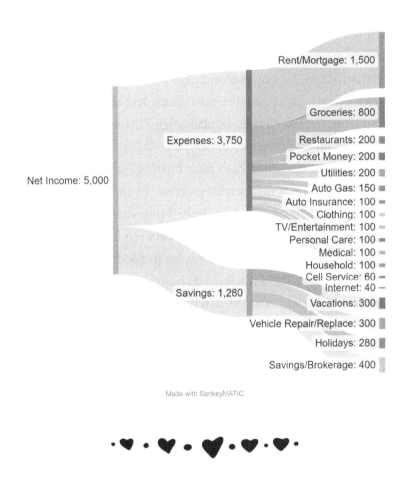

Made with SankeyMATIC

Rent/Mortgage: 1,500
Groceries: 800
Expenses: 3,750
Restaurants: 200
Pocket Money: 200
Utilities: 200
Net Income: 5,000
Auto Gas: 150
Auto Insurance: 100
Clothing: 100
TV/Entertainment: 100
Personal Care: 100
Medical: 100
Household: 100
Cell Service: 60
Internet: 40
Savings: 1,280
Vacations: 300
Vehicle Repair/Replace: 300
Holidays: 280
Savings/Brokerage: 400

Cash Flow Timing

One problem you may have is the *timing* of the cash flow. What if all the bills (or the biggest ones) are due at the start of the month? You can solve that in a few ways. One is to build up a cash buffer in your checking account, but it might take time if you're starting from tapped out. A quicker method would be to contact anyone you're making payments to and ask to have your payment dates moved to the end of the month, or strategically spread through the month. Most will cooperate. Be persistent. Ask for a manager, as the first-line customer service reps have little power to do things like that. Maybe lay out a second page with a timeline of when to pay for everything, so you don't overdraw. You have that overdraft setup from the last chapter in place, right? At least the start of it with a few hundred bucks?

What about those big cash flow busting bubble months like in the summer, when you take vacation, or the end of the year, when all those holidays roll around? How about this—suppose you typically spend $1,500 each year between Thanksgiving and the other end-of-year holidays. Factor in food, travel, gifts, the whole shebang. What if you started an automatic transfer of $125 a month to a holiday savings virtual bucket in January? Guess what? When it's time to spend that money, it's there waiting for you, with accumulated interest! Boom, even better than an interest-free loan. Just transfer it to your checking account. No need to jack up the credit cards, and have to look at them with sadness and regret after the holidays are over. Do the same for vacations, car repairs, and any other big event you need to pay for in the future.

Another way to keep this all organized is to pay your bills from one place, usually your bank's bill pay page. Then you can see the sequence of what's getting paid when, and control it better. This is much harder if you're giving out your card or bank info to every single utility and person you pay a bill to and letting them pull it out willy-nilly. Maintain control yourself and put as much as you can on auto-pilot.

Another problem is variable income. Some folks don't get a regular paycheck—they rely on tips, commissions, business income, or other types of uneven cash income. If this is the case, just take your best guess at what next month's income will be. Try to be conservative—if you beat the number, it's gravy. The emergency fund and buffer in your checking account are more important in cases like this, so beef it up as soon as possible. Then you can borrow from yourself to cover the slow periods. We'll show you a better way to fill this gap in the chapter on earning more.

Alright, got cash-flow fever? It's not that hard. It's liberating. Often, while doing this, people find so much wasted money it's like a new paycheck. Just rinse and repeat the exercise toward the end of each month with anyone else that's part of your team. Review how you did in the current month and set up the next one. It's your monthly 30-minute family finance board meeting. You can hash out any discussions, and then you're done fighting about money for another month. You're on the path to a life where there's only joy around your money, nothing to fight about, the biggest challenge being what to do with it all and how to pay fewer taxes on it! (Yeah, we'll cover that, too.)

Okie dokie. Ready to learn how to get that money rolling in?

"Do not save what is left after spending; instead spend what is left after saving."

Warren Buffett

CHAPTER THREE

Making More Moolah

SHOW ME THE MONEY!

"Money, if it does not bring you happiness, will at least help you be miserable in comfort."
Helen Gurley Brown

There are *so* many ways to make more money! But not all of them are right for you. Let's find some you'll enjoy. I'll break this very important chapter into sections. First, a little job/career advice. Then, we'll talk about ways to find easy money—money under rocks with your name on them! After that, we'll discuss starting a small business. Finally, we'll close with the myriad side hustles out there (or in your own home!).

On the Job

In my corporate career, I sat behind the desk for countless hiring interviews and performance reviews. I know that side of the desk very well. It's important for you to know it too, because that knowledge is a valuable bargaining chip. First, if you were going to sell your car (we'll get to know how to do that later!), you'd probably start with a quick search to find out what it's worth. Common sense, right? The thing is, most folks don't know what they, themselves, are worth in the job marketplace! At least once a year, and certainly prior to your performance review, check job market sites like glassdoor.com, salary.com, or payscale.com to see what other companies in your area (and your company) are offering for people with your experience in your position. You might even see that your company is trying to entice new hires with pay rates higher than yours. Them's fighting words!

Look, your employer doesn't want to lose you. It's very expensive to hire a replacement and train them. It takes time, and newbies often make expensive mistakes. Use that to your advantage. If you don't feel you're fairly compensated (or just want to take a shot at a raise/bonus), be upfront about it.

"I love working here, but to be honest, my family is growing, inflation is hurting our quality of life, and I'm struggling with these student loans. I was poking around on some sites and saw the marketplace is paying more than what I'm making. Can you do better? I'd love to stay."

Perfectly acceptable, as long as it's delivered professionally and not with menace or as a threat. You can only get away with maybe one of these a year, so make it count. As a manager, I was often told to inform employees "things are tight" and "there's not much money for raises or bonuses." That's bull. The money is always there—for the employees that come to their performance reviews well-armed with job marketplace facts and a well-documented list of their accomplishments throughout the year. Each time you filled in for someone else, worked extra hours, mentored someone new, all that. The squeaky wheel gets the grease. The raise/bonus money magically appears. They don't want to lose you! Work on that accomplishments list all year round, while your good deeds are top of mind. If you wait until the day before your performance review to build your list of annual accomplishments, it's going to be incomplete and suck. Your manager will be able to tell. Not a good look for your organizational skills!

What else can you do? Improve yourself. You are your product. Improve and enhance that product. You, version 2.0. Take an interest in facets of the company outside your own responsibilities. Learn how things work. Think about jumping on a self-paced e-learning site like coursera.org or udemy.com and getting a process or project management certificate. Those are valuable for promotions and on your resume! It's a good, inexpensive investment even if you pay for it yourself. Always ask your employer to reimburse you. At the least, it puts your initiative and new skills on their radar. Some people whine their employer is taking advantage of them. Flip the tables, use them to climb the ladder, as a stepping-stone to a better career doing what you enjoy for more reward. Listen, you can be one of those people always complaining that life happens to them, or do something about it. If you are, stop thinking and saying that. It's holding you back. Murphy visits all of us.

There are tons of career-change opportunities that don't require college and can be done with a quick certificate. There are great, free programs like theamericandreamacademy.org, sponsored by big corporations (see, they're not all that bad...). If you hate your current career, reinvent yourself (at any age).

Case Study: I had a client who was a long-haul trucker, and dog tired of it. He wanted more time at home with his kids. The job was tearing up his body and soul. I advised him to take a safety officer training course and approach his management about it. By the end of our time together, he was strutting around the depot in his flashy safety officer neon vest, working 9-5, going home to dinner, and sleeping in his own bed.

Case Study: I had a young client who was working in a nearby cement plant. He hadn't any education past high school and believed his options for career change were limited. We explored and discovered he liked puzzles, which shows an aptitude for tech. Within six months, he had his official Google IT Tech certificate and now can't wait to get to work every day in his tech job.

When you're looking for a job, try alternative or newer sites like flexjobs.com, snagajob.com, or usajobs.gov.

Easy Money

I mentioned finding easy money under rocks with your name on them. Here are a few ideas.

Unclaimed Money. If you're owed money from a past insurance settlement, rebate, class action lawsuit, tax refund, deposit, inheritance, or other reason, and they can't track you down, those folks can't just keep that money. They have to file with the state of your last known address. Use legit sites like unclaimed.org, mi ssingmoney.com, or usa.gov/unclaimed-money. Don't just search and find a site as there are many scams in this area. Also, don't do a lazy nationwide search. Search for your name in each state you have lived in. While you're there, check for any friends or relatives and see if they'll give you a finder's fee!

W4. Do you get a big tax refund every year? That's just plain silly. Why loan that much-needed money to the government each year interest-free when you could and should get a bigger paycheck each month? Get with your HR or payroll department and update your W4 form. It results in more positive cash flow each month to pay off debt or invest!

Deductions. While we're on the paycheck topic, actually sit down and read your paystub. Make sure you know what each deduction from your hard-earned gross pay is for. Sometimes it's random, useless, or unnecessary stuff. Call payroll and have those canceled! Voila, more positive cash flow each month.

Sick/Paid Time Off. Been piling up those hours? It should also be on your paystub. See if your employer will buy it back from you. Many do. Bingo—extra money!

Old Savings Bonds. Back in the day, when a child was born, family members would buy paper savings bonds. They would get tucked away in sock drawers or a safe and forgotten. Nowadays they still do, but people buy electronic savings bonds. Ask your parents, grandparents, or others if they have anything like this with your name on it.

Coins. Time to breakout those jugs of old coins you've been collecting. Check them for any that might be valuable, then cash them all in and make an extra payment on your smallest debt, or buy a share of a great index fund (we'll cover that later).

Old 401k/Pensions. Call any old employer HR departments and see if they have any old retirement plan money for you, or even awarded company stock. It could be worth way more now than it was back then! Some of these may show up under the missing money step.

Taxes. Review your past three years of returns and see if you missed any deductions. It's pretty easy these days to file an amended return and get a sweet check on the way to you. **Old Gift Cards.** Check around your house. You can sell these on online marketplaces like giftcardgranny.com. **Sell/Rent Other Crap.** You can sell or rent almost anything in your house, garage, basement, closets these days. Get busy and build up an online market at nextdoor.com, craigslist.org, Facebook Marketplace, and other sites. Go all Marie Kondo on that old clutter! People buy broken and obsolete stuff because there's a market for the parts, or they strip out any valuable metals using special equipment. If you have six items for sale, not much will happen. If you have dozens, there will be regular activity. Some specialized marketplaces are gazelle.com and swappa.com for phones/electronics, worthy.com for jewelery, and mercari.com, p oshmark.com, thredup.com, and therealreal.com for clothing. You can rent your car on sites like turo.com and getaround.com, RV on rvshare.com, your backyard pool on swimply.com, and just about anything else on fatllama.com.

Case Study. I had a client whose kids had grown up and weren't using the swimming pool in his backyard much. He listed it for rent at swimply.com and had a fun summer hosting birthday parties for kids each weekend. You can also turn your backyard into a dog park and rent it out. The options are unlimited, get creative! Most of these listing sites cover insurance, collecting payments, etc. Easy-peasy.

Sell Plasma (or Other Body Stuff). Often the places that buy plasma offer big bonuses. They're clean and well-run, with children's play areas. Check reviews first, though. Nothing like sitting in a comfy chair listening to music for half an hour and getting paid! It's good for your health and helps others in need. The money is also tax free, a tremendous bonus! Also, check into selling other body stuff (yeah, it's a thing...). There's a guy who makes $180k a year selling his poop to humanmicrobes.org because he has some special kind. Crazy. Take part in clinical trials at your local doctor's office or other medical facility. Some of those are super easy, such as sleep studies. What's easier than making money when you're sleeping or pooping? I digest.

Cash Value/Permanent Life Insurance or Annuities. These are mostly risky, overpriced, fee-laden garbage (we'll explain why later). If you really need life insurance, get an inexpensive term policy in place, then cash these out and pay off your debt or invest the lump sum. Winning!

Credit Card Rebates. I ranted on this in the last two chapters, so please go back and read those sections again. That said, if you really are into this challenge and enjoy it, it can be a side hustle like the others. Just make sure you're paying that card off every month to keep your monthly cash flow clean, and have a big emergency fund to not get caught in the trap the banks know will eventually spring on you. Make no mistake—despite the claims from the influencers on social media about how great and easy this is, it can be hard work tracking the cards, when the promos expire, and so forth. I don't recommend it. The "rewards" are becoming harder to use and coming with more restrictions and stipulations. They can yank those benefits at any time.

Side Hustles

As I said when discussing missing money, be careful here. If you just randomly search the internet for side hustles, you'll likely be confronted with pages of scams and multi-level marketing (MLM) schemes. MLMs are fine if you are a highly persuasive sales type who doesn't mind when your friends, relatives, and coworkers all run when they see you coming. Many are just scams. You can do better. Avoid anything that wants you to spend money up-front for inventory, classes, etc. There are reviews and updates at sites like sidehustlenation.com and budgetsaresexy.com. We teach a private virtual class on this with specific examples and personalized help at emancipare.com.

Don't forget—if you're doing any of these, you can write off any related expenses, up to how much you made. That often includes things like your internet service, cell phones, home office space, and much more. It's one of the hidden bonuses! As you get rolling, it's highly recommended to set up a separate business checking account and debit card, so your income and expenses are clear at tax time.

I'm going to list a ton of side hustles here. Go through the list and pick out some candidates that are a good match with your hobbies or passions—things you actually like to do. Also, you want to have two categories of side hustles. Pick a few that are like money faucets—you can set up quickly, then turn them on and off when you need a quick few bucks to fill in a hole in your budget for the month, or replenish your emergency fund. Pick a few that might be a slower burn to get set up and started, but are candidates for a legit long-term small business. We'll cover how to set that up at the end of this chapter.

Also, don't get frustrated by low pay rates or dribbling income when you start. Be persistent! As you get better and better, as you learn the ropes, the trickle turns into a stream and maybe a geyser of cash. Some of these service providers will start you out low as a trial period, but pay you more as you prove your worth.

Side Hustles from Home

Stuff Flipper. If you took our advice above and cleaned out your garage, basement, closets to sell stuff online, you already have a finely tuned system set up. Maybe you enlisted the help of family members and everyone has a job in that process. If you did well, you're out of stuff to sell! Now build on that by going to local yard/garage sales, flea markets, estate sales, Salvation Army, Goodwill, and Habitat for Humanity stores looking for prime items to buy on the cheap, clean up, and flip online for a big profit. Check your local newspaper's bargain bin classified section. Dumpster-dive at local apartment complexes or dormitories. You can even set up your own specialty stores at places like Amazon or eBay for books, golf supplies, and just about anything else.

Blog/Write/Podcast. If you're passionate about a particular subject and like to create content, start a blog, podcast, or self-published book. Book publishing is cheap and easy at Amazon Kindle's kdp.com. Remember when we heard the first inklings of news about a virus spreading in China back in 2019? Some enterprising folks did quick searching and put together 99-cent booklets on how to keep your family safe from COVID, publishing them on Amazon within days and using the free covers and resources available. Guess how many of those they were selling per day when the pandemic hit peak world-wide spread and everyone in the world panicked? Once you create the content, it's easy to re-use it as a blog (wordpress.org, wix.com, weebly.com), podcast (just do the audio recording and post on podbean.com), a YouTube channel, and so forth. You make money by using affiliate links and hosting advertisements on your content for blogs/podcasts/YouTube channels and from royalties on self-publishing platforms.

Case Study: A burned-out IT manager client had a passion for horseback riding and liked to write. I helped her set up a blog on all things equestrian, as well as affiliate accounts at online stores like Tractor Supply and Amazon. Each time she blogged about an equestrian product she loved, people clicked those links to buy and she received commission—not just on the product, but everything they bought in that shopping session! Pays big during the holidays. Use tools like Yoast SEO to gain traction.

Book Proofreader/Reviewer/Cover Designer. Like to read? Set up an account at sites like Fiverr or Upwork as a book reviewer or beta reader. There are millions of self-published indie (independent) authors that use these services. Specialize in the genre of books you like to read! If you're good with art, design their covers for them.

Photography: There are many sites online to sell your pictures, such as foap.com, istock.com, and depositphotos.com. People buy them for their websites, to create book covers, and many other uses.

Case Study: I had a client who was out of work during the pandemic. She said she liked photography and had a good camera, but wasn't a "professional." I had her get some inexpensive business cards printed up and told her to hand them to anyone that came within arm's reach, and tell them she takes photos of kids and pets. Can't go wrong there! After a year of that, she had graduated to doing weddings and big events. No more bartending for that young lady!

Auto Detailing. Set up shop in your driveway with some basic tools and a calendar scheduling service like calendly.com. Work your way up and someday you might do this full-time with your own van or location.

Be an Expert. Sites like JustAnswer.com allow you to answer questions in many areas and get paid for it. I had a nurse client who was making $1,500 a month answering questions from nursing school students on a platform like this.

Personal Care. Do child or adult care with an account at car e.com or sittercity.com. You can pick the age ranges if you don't want to change diapers. Likely requires certification.

Pet Care. Walk your neighbors' dogs, feed them, sit for them on sites like dogvacay.com, wag.com, rover.com.

Notary. Take a class at one of the online learning sites I mentioned earlier and get certified by your state. Set up an online booking calendar (calendly.com) with your available hours.

Teaching/Tutoring. Get paid to share your lifetime of knowledge! A lot of this happens online now and runs the gamut from teaching foreign kids English as a second language to helping US kids with subjects they're struggling with. You don't need a teaching certificate in most cases.

Consulting. Leverage your expertise again to do consulting from home at sites like freelancer.com or wahve.com.

Medical Claims Coding. Insurance companies will often provide training and a laptop to do this work at home part-time.

Roommates/Renters. Sites like silvernest.com use dating-service like algorithms to find the perfect person to rent that spare bedroom, mother-daughter suite, garage apartment, or other space. They take care of background checks and collecting payments.

Type. Transcribe audio files to text at sites like rev.com.

Sell. Be an at-home customer service rep for companies like QVC and Home Shopping Network at sites like liveops.com or nextrep.com.

Jury Duty. Be a practice juror for attorneys at sites like ejury.com, virtualjury.com, and onlineverdict.com.

Cook. Teach cooking or host dinner parties at sites like cozymeal.com or eatwith.com.

Research. Do phone surveys and research at sites like fancyhands.com. Join a consumer focus group.

Craft. Sell your unique crafts or other personalized items at etsy.com. Be creative!

Case Study: A young relative was driving his parents nuts with his new 3D printer, consuming materials and printing out crazy stuff. He started making spurs for the Crocks footwear and it became a thing on etsy.com. Soon, he had multiple printers running and had to enlist the help of his school friends to keep up. By senior year in high school, he had purchased a new Tesla for himself. He has zero artistic or craft skill. Anything is possible. Be in an entrepreneurial mindset and always looking around you for the next big viral trend (see: fidget spinners).

Side Hustles Outside Home

Drive. uber.com and lyft.com are the obvious choices here. You can just turn the app on when you have some free time, and putter around the house until a prospective ride pops up, then decide to take it or not based on the location and rider profile. It's a fun way to meet people and you get lots of tax writeoffs for mileage, car washes, and supplies! Deliver packages with courier sites like roadie.com. Get paid to advertise during your commute with wr apify.com or carvertise.com. Drive a school bus or shuttle for the local senior homes or rehabilitation facilities.

Note: When using your car for side hustles, it's important to check with your auto insurance company to ensure you're covered. Sometimes they don't cover that activity, but the companies (such as Uber and Lyft) will pick up the slack. Make sure there aren't any exposed gaps where you're not protected.

Deliver. Grab food for folks at sites like ubereats.com, doordash.com, grubhub.com. Go old-school and call your local restaurants and see if they're hiring a part-time delivery driver. Get up early and throw newspapers out your car window for the local newspaper.

Shop. Deliver groceries, food, and other household goods using sites like shipt.com, peapod.com, and instacart.com.

Services. Be your own geek squad with hellotech.com. Be a mobile mechanic at yourmechanic.com. Cook at locations with feastly.com. Do hair/nails with beglammed.com. Do home/property maintenance with taskeasy.com, lawnlove.com, handy.com, or thumbtack.com. Give out samples at sites like productionsplus.com. Join a street team marketing group to have fun at festivals and events. Do modeling (even if you don't look like J-Lo or A-Rod) at local schools for art or photography students. Run our own local tour business at sites like toursbylocals.com.

Mobile Notary. Take that home notary business from the in-home side hustle list above on the road and make up to $100/hour.

Random. Look, it can be as simple as going to a site like wonolo.com or snagajob.com/shifts/workers on a slow weeknight or weekend and picking up a fun, local four or eight-hour shift at a local Amazon distribution point or other employer needing quick temp help. These are often social environments and you get paid right away.

These are just some examples. I could fill an entire book just with side hustles. They come and go, so if links don't work, be persistent. There are so many options, it's hard to imagine there's not something ideal for you in that long list. Get to it. Turn those money faucets on and prosper. Be an entrepreneur. Show your kids there are options other than the hamster wheel in life.

Side Hustle Resources

This is an ever-changing landscape, with new side-hustles popping up all the time, and some providers disappearing or merging into others. Stay on top of the scene at sites like sidehustlenation.com and budgetsaresexy.com. J. Money, a skateboarding, Mohawk-styled blogger, runs the latter site.

Starting a Business

As I said earlier, some of the above choices, especially if they're things you enjoy, can turn into full-fledged businesses after a while. You may start cutting yourself a regular paycheck, starting a generous solo 401k and health insurance plan for yourself, and hiring employees. Maybe, just maybe, quitting that job you hate going to. You get the tax write-offs for everyday expenses, and more.

It's not that hard. The minute you do any side hustle, you are a small business, a sole proprietor by default. That means you file a simple schedule C with your federal taxes, which lists your income and expense totals. You can use a name other than your own by filing a "doing business as" form with your state. Later, if things pick up, you can turn the business into a limited liability company

(LLC) for more benefits. It's easy to do on your own at your state small business portal. Don't pay services like LegalZoom to do it. You're the boss. You can decide to only work four days a week, or take the summers off, or whatever you want to do.

Get a business checking account and debit card to keep everything separate. When you need accounting, free services like Wave Accounting work well. You can get an inexpensive business email address and register your domain at domains.google.com. Take advantage of the free, taxpayer-funded resources at score.org and americassbdc.org, as well as the Veteran's Administration if you're a vet like me (and, thank you!). Get any insurance you might need.

You're now fully armed with ways to make more money, even if you're stuck in the house with a bunch of kids. There's always time, and there are no more excuses. Let's move on to the other big part of this equation—how to save money on just about everything.

CHAPTER FOUR

Pay Less for Everything

BE A SMART CONSUMER

*"The best way to look stylish on a budget is to try
second-hand, bargain hunting, and vintage."*
Orlando Bloom

We'll get into the details in this chapter later for things like groceries, restaurants, and so forth. But first, let's talk about the war on you. Who's making war on you? The army of psychologists, sociologists, and marketers hired by the big companies. Their job is to convince and coerce you to buy things you don't need without thinking. They love that impulse purchase. They drive and inspire your YOLO, FOMO, and need for status. It's their whispers you hear in your ear or brain, via many subtle methods. "You deserve this." They are the enemy of your financial freedom and happiness. They spend billions of dollars a year on these goals.

A common tactic is to remove friction. Amazon figured out a long time ago that causing you to take multiple steps to purchase something (add stuff to cart, go to cart, give address, give payment method...) was just giving you lots of opportunity to bail out. They devised the magical Buy It Now button, which you can click and have the item on its way to you. Card charged, no friction. They took it a step further by selling little quarter-sized buttons to stick up around your house. Those connect to your Wi-Fi and allow you to order a fresh box of your favorite crackers or jug of laundry detergent in an instant. You don't even need to open your computer or phone. Be wary of anything that wants you to act without thinking.

When you walk into the grocery store during the holidays and spot the Christmas tree made up of two-liter bottles of Coke, it's not there because the store manager is in a festive mood. Coke pays for that "product placement" because they know you're probably hosting company and will need soft drinks. They want you to load up now, before you get to the soft drink aisle and spot all the lower-priced competition. When you check out, that brightly lit and overpriced display of candy is there because the store knows you've been looking at food for an hour and probably starving by now. Especially the kids, if they're with you.

Brands pay more to get their products placed at eye level. Look up or down to find the less expensive alternatives who aren't paying all that money! Often, the expensive big-name companies make store brands for the grocery chains. There's no difference, other than the price being way cheaper because of saving millions of dollars in advertising and commercials. I bet you can't taste the difference in almost all cases.

Any time you reach for something to buy, or reach for your card, or browsing online, get in the habit of asking yourself a question. ***"Do I want this more than my freedom?"***
I've seen folks go in for an oil change and get enticed into buying a new car that meant they'd have to work ten or more years. Is a new car worth that? By the way, this is why oil changes are so cheap at the dealership (not really, as in this case, they can cost over $30,000). Find a good, ethical local mechanic if your car is out of warranty.

A key part of getting the best deals on everything is to develop a strategy for quickly determining which products are the best ones for the least money. Some people trust a certain brand name. That doesn't really work. Viking makes great stoves, but their $10,000 refrigerator was rated one of the worst products ever. You could have bought a far better one for a fraction of the price. All car manufacturers make some good cars and some clunkers. Even a specific model may be good during one redesign, and bad coming out of the next one. Some people say "I always buy everything at Walmart, they're the cheapest." Not really. A Hallmark or American Greetings card will cost you $7 there, same as in the expensive boutique store in the mall, because those companies don't let Walmart discount their products. You can get the same Hallmark or American Greetings card at the dollar store for a buck, though! Ok, maybe $1.25 these days.

So, how can you tell where the best buys are? You can't really trust reviews as much anymore, since folks gamed the ones on Amazon and other sites. They can be useful if you filter out ones from outside countries, and be sure to always read the negative ones, not just the "stuffed-in" glowing ones. I like to find trusted, objective sources. The best one ever is consumerreports.org. They take no advertising and test the heck out of products. I get their magazine, but the real bonus is in their app and browser plugin. If I'm looking at toasters online, it will pop up and say something like, "Hey, that one you're looking at sucks, but here are three that are less expensive and came in at the top of our ratings." Boom! When in the stores, I often use their app or website to look products up.

I'll list some additional strategies below.

Never go shopping just to see "what they have." C'mon now. Find something better to do if you're bored. Hit up that side hustle! Always make a targeted shopping list, go in the store with blinders on, get what you need, and get the heck out. Be strategic.

Trial Hack. If there are several products or services you're considering, sign up for the free or discounted trial for each one in turn. Put the trial end date on your calendar and cancel before it ends and they charge you! Then sign up for the next one. A little organization with this hack can save you tons. Sometimes, by the time you get to the end of the list, the first ones are begging you to come back with further discounts! We'll give examples later in this chapter.

Don't fall for fake sales. Stores often start at the "regular" price for something, then jack it up over a few months, only to have a magical "40% off" sale that just brings it back to the regular price. But, it entices unknowing consumers out to buy boatloads. Some good sales are at the end of a season. For example, when Costco or Lowe's want to get rid of the big patio items so they don't have to store them all winter. If you buy something, keep scanning circulars or online to see whether it's gone on sale after that, then go to the store and demand some money back.

There's no such thing as 0% financing. Nobody loans money for free. Nobody (well, except maybe your mom). Why would they do that when they could invest it or put it in the bank and earn interest? When you buy something at 0% financing, the interest is actually baked into the price. That's even worse than regular interest, because the rate is hidden! When I negotiate new car prices and they pull this on me, I later inform the salesperson that I'm paying cash, and suddenly the price comes down by thousands of dollars. That was the "free" 0% interest coming off.

Don't lease or buy extended warranties. Leasing (especially with cars) is the most expensive way to own something. The lower payments are just an illusion. They'll get you later. Count on it. If you're buying quality products, as I'm advocating, you no longer need extended warranties. They're often full of loopholes and a waste of money.

Buy dinged up. Some folks, once they decide which toaster they want, will search for a box on the shelf that's dinged up. They'll then march to the customer service counter and ask for a discount. And they'll get it. We often buy floor models of items at huge discounts, because they're "open box" and sometimes have a slight blemish or missing the manual (get it online).

Buy local. Before you spend hundreds on a new lawn mower or other expensive item, see if anyone in your area is selling one that's like new for a fraction of the price. Check the usual places—Facebook Marketplace, nextdoor.com, craigslist.org, yard sales, garage sales. Huge savings!

Online Used Marketplaces. Phones and electronics at sites like gazelle.com or swappa.com, clothing at sites like mercari.com, poshmark.com, and therealreal.com. The options are endless for lovingly used but like-new products at a fraction of the cost. ebay.com is the old-school go-to.

Buy at big box stores. A membership at Costco, Sam's Club, or BJs costs money but can result in huge savings. We love Costco! The big savings on quality products (especially the Kirkland store brand) adds up. Guess who makes the delicious Kirkland coffee we enjoy? Starbucks. Tuna? Bumblebee. Batteries? Duracell. You get those top brands and quality for fractions of the cost. Their tires, pharmacy, optical, hearing, vacations, and other specialty departments can save you big money.

Dollar stores. Hit them up as your go-to!

Waste not, want not. Next time you're about to throw away a used-up tube of toothpaste, cut it open with a razor knife (careful!). Lookie there—a few weeks of toothpaste (even if you used one of those roller gadgets). Same with about any non-transparent consumer goods container. Be gazelle-intense on not wasting. It makes an enormous difference over the years! If we use a paper plate for chips or something, I'll often brush it off and put it back in the package. Please don't tell Ms. Emancipare!

Consumer savings weapons. I love joinhoney.com because it always has those secret coupon/discount codes when I'm checking out online. One time I was buying $250 worth of blinds and it took $50 off. Bazinga! I like to use keyringapp.com to electronically store and organize all those pesky bar-code key fob plastic thingies for shopping discounts. I save my other cards there too, like AAA and AARP. But I wouldn't use it for anything sensitive, like a driver's license or a Medicare card.

Always, always ask. "Do you have any group/association discounts?" "Can you do better than that?" "Can you take something off? This seems damaged." "Do I want this more than my freedom?"

Groceries

This is a big monthly expense, especially for larger families. Stock up on what you can at the big box stores I just talked about, especially when things are on sale. I wait until something like my antacid is on sale at Costco, buy six months worth, then not buy again until it goes on sale again. It's a double win, since it's already cheap there, plus the sale price! Few folks snip coupons these days, but you can use sites like ibotta.com snipsnap.com, and coupon sherpa.com to save money. Don't fall for gimmicks like "Five for $10." Often, you can buy just one or two and get the same sale price. It's just a psych gimmick to get you to buy more.

Try to use the same chain for groceries and work that store loyalty card hard. Take advantage of the free ham or turkey around the holidays or gas discounts. When comparing products, a good way to see which is the best value is looking at the cost per unit, not the price. Don't get sucked in by the pretty packages—the ugly package store brands are much cheaper and often just as good or better. Think about using those misfit produce websites. Does it matter what a potato looks like if you'll be peeling and mashing it? You might find one that looks like a celebrity and post it to go viral and make you a celebrity. Don't go too crazy with organic for things that get peeled, like bananas and oranges.

The number one way to save on groceries is to pay attention when checking out and always check your receipt! I always, always find problems where I bought something because it was on sale, but the sale price hadn't been entered in the computer. Or, the clerk at the register weighed my boring yellow onions and then rang them up as imported Vidalia onions at 3x the price. Or rang my five gallon Deer Park water jug up as a new purchase without a returned empty, costing me $8 more! The staff is overworked, underpaid, and stressed. Do self-checkout to avoid problems like this. Check your receipts for double-charges and missed sales prices.

The other huge savings on groceries is by making sure not to waste food. In the US, it's estimated the average household wastes

40% or more of their food. Make something out of the leftovers. Make smaller portions. Sometimes, especially for smaller families, grabbing the pre-prepared meals to go from the deli area is a better option. They're freshly prepared and just need to be heated at home. It saves time and waste from food prep, and is healthier than frozen food.

Another way to avoid waste, especially for couples or small families, is to use meal kit services like homechef.com, hellofresh.com, and many others. They seem expensive at first blush, but consider there's no waste, and you're saving time, gas/vehicle wear and tear, and money planning meals and shopping. It's fun to pick out the meals for the next week, and the food is top quality and delicious based on the ones we've tried. Employ the "trial hack" mentioned above to cycle through them all for months, saving tons on food and eating like kings and queens. You might find a favorite and stick with it.

Restaurants

First, consider alternatives like the meal kits and fresh to-go meals discussed under the grocery topic above. Or, get your restaurant meals to-go and save on the beverages and desserts that are massively overpriced, plus tips. Another hack is to go in the late afternoon if possible, when the lower lunch pricing is in place. Apps like groupon.com and restaurant.com can save a ton as well. If you have kids, go on "kids eat free" nights at popular chains.

Develop a habit where each time you're dining out, when the server comes over to ask if you'd like to see the dessert menu (meaning they're getting ready to total you up), ask "Do you have any discounts for veterans, health care workers, AARP or AAA members, or workers at my company?" It never hurts to ask. I've had servers say, "No, but my manager says if anyone asks, to just take 10% off." Never be afraid to ask. The difference over a lifetime is huge.

Transportation

We'll talk about buying and selling vehicles later, but here's a preview—never lease a car, under normal circumstances. Yes, there are folks that get ridiculously good deals because they work for car manufacturers, or subsidies from their employers. Normal people shouldn't lease cars. Yes, the payments look sweet compared to loan payments. They'll ding you later, don't worry.

The first big hack in saving on transportation costs would be to have fewer vehicles. Since covid, when employers finally woke up to the fact that people actually work more when they work from home, that's where many people work. So do you still need two cars? Consider how many times there are actual conflicts, and whether using an inexpensive ride-share or car-share service would fix those occasional problems. Or a short, cheap rental for a weekend trip. It's a lot cheaper than paying for insurance, registration, repairs, and all the other year-round costs of owning a vehicle.

The second big hack, of course, is always paying cash for vehicles. A big car payment is the biggest avoidable obstacle to your financial happiness and independence. Dude, it's just a way to get from one place to another, and grandma or some runny-nose-brat is gonna ding it up on you, anyway. There are countless memes about getting rich by driving a crappy car, and they're true. All those silent, anonymous millionaires next door do it. Many of the folks driving the flashy, big-payment status symbols have been my clients, I promise. And they ain't happy.

Ok. sermon over. Back to reality. The top way to save on gas is to properly inflate your tires. Buy an inexpensive digital tire gauge, they're cool to use and it only takes a sec to check. Lighten your ride to save more gas, and take any non-aerodynamic accessories off when you aren't using them (bike racks, roof racks, the ornamental reindeer's antlers you still have on your hood). Shut that thing off when you're waiting for junior to come out of hockey practice. You can still listen to the radio on accessory mode without burning gas. Get a used EV or plug-in hybrid—I love mine! Be picky about where you buy your gas. Places like Costco have great quality gas for a good price. Use your supermarket points for discounts. Some of the big-name oil companies charge outrageous prices for basically the same product, despite the gimmicky ads about "superior performance." When you use your phone GPS software to set up a route, pay attention to the alternate routes it's showing that may have lower or no tolls (and a more scenic route that will save on gas since you won't be going 80 MPH on the super-slab!).

Want to know the best way to save money on transportation? Develop a relationship (keep it clean, now) with an honest local mechanic. As always, use Google and Yelp reviews and look for the keywords – honest, ethical, etc. Read the critical reviews, if there are any. If you get someone like that on a first-name basis, they can save you countless money over the course of your driving life. When you go to buy a new-to-you car, they can run it through the paces and find problems that are well hidden. They'll even know which customers are getting ready to sell good used cars and tip you off. If you're buying a new car, they'll tell you which ones suck. Most of all, they won't tell you your cabin filter needs to be replaced, then charge you $50 to do it like a dealer, when you can buy one for $5 at Walmart and replace it easily yourself (hint: it's in the glove box). Use sites like repairpal.com, Consumer Reports, and AAA to find out what the going rate is for different repairs in your area. If you want work done at your home or work parking lot, try yourmechanic.com.

The best bang for your buck for high-quality tires are the big box stores (Costco, et al.) or tirerack.com online (you can have them shipped directly to your local mechanic to install or have yourmechanic.com do it at your home or work).

Home Utilities

Turn stuff off when you aren't using it! Not so fast, you say. These days, when you turn most electronics off, they just go into standby mode (to listen to and report your conversations to marketers). You can buy special power strips that actually sense standby mode and cut power completely. It can save you on electricity and enhance privacy. Use sleep timers if you (or the kids) like watching television or listening to music to fall asleep. You'll sleep better! But yeah, turn off those lights when you're leaving a room (as long as your significant other isn't still in there) and don't watch your water run down the drain while you're brushing your teeth. Imagine it as money going down the drain, literally.

Smart thermostats have a huge return on investment by cutting the heat or air when you're snug in bed. They make sure the temp is just right by the time you wake. Some come with apps so you can turn the usage down while you're away, and turn it back on when you're on the way home. That's big savings on heat and AC! Use an incense stick on a windy day to check for leaks in the seams around your doors and windows. Order a free consumer kit to fix those from your gas or electric company (or both). Wrap your pipes with insulation and always fix any leaking faucets, toilets, showers immediately. Your sewer bill is often tied to your water usage, you get nailed twice for excess! Speaking of water, most people have their hot water heater turned up way too high. Back it down a little each day until you find the sweet spot (that would be when your partner screams at you during their shower).

Call your utility companies and ask to be put on the monthly budget plan. They'll look at your year-long usage and charge you an average each month. It makes budgeting really easy! Make sure your clothes dryer lint trap *and* the hoses leading away from it are clear. Clogs make them run longer and could cause a fire. Run your big appliances on a delay timer or schedule to kick off late at night, when your electricity rate should be lower. Wash small loads of dishes by hand (Yeah, I've seen the "research" sponsored by the dishwasher companies, that only talk about water usage and don't factor in the thing is running for 90 minutes on electricity).

Switch your light bulbs to LEDs. They last longer and use less electricity for a brighter light. You should also make sure your ceiling fans rotate in the correct way each season. Clockwise (looking up at it) in the winter, and counter-clockwise in the summer. Put them on slow speed to more evenly circulate the heat or AC around the house. Yes, it uses more juice, but in most cases, it's a positive return on your investment.

Solar panels can be an excellent investment *if* your home is situated properly. Don't lease them, buy them. Don't put them on a roof that's close to needing to be replaced. Add them to your homeowner's coverage. The payback for this expense is growing shorter and shorter, but do the math, especially if you're considering moving. Be careful—there are a ton of solar scammers.

Internet

Most people are oversold bandwidth and pay for way more than they need. Unless you have a house full of gamers, 250Mbps is a good place to start. That's what we use, and we're often streaming news channels and on meetings all day. If you have dead spots in basements, attics, decks, or other faraway places, get some highly rated internet extender devices. It's a one-time purchase and they work great. Don't fix that problem by overcompensating with an expensive internet speed. Think about buying your own modem instead of renting from the internet company.

Most people aren't getting what they're paying for! Run speed test.net every once in a while and make sure you are. If not, call them and demand a pro-rated refund for the service you've been paying for, and ask them to fix it. Often the modem needs a patch or fix, or just a reboot. We have a small timer plug on our modem that turns it off and back on each night at 3am. That helps with the unavoidable gumming up that happens after they've been running for a long time.

Make sure you're getting subsidy help from your employer if you're working at home, and if you're doing one of those sweet side hustles from the last chapter, write it off!

Entertainment

The best entertainment value by far is your local library. What a wonderful, old-school place to go hang out, stress free, and enjoy books, audiobooks, movies, magazines, video games, and so much more for *free*. You can also get most resources online. Support your local library! If you like to read books, sites like booksiren s.com and netgalley.com will give you all you can read for free, if you're willing to post reviews. As we discussed in the last chapter, you can get paid for that, too!

Be careful with SiriusXM! They're notorious for sending you renewal notices for hundreds of dollars for just six months. Bull. I promptly call them and tell them I'm canceling and going with the free, excellent tunein.com (it uses cell data when driving, but most people are on unlimited plans now). The Sirius phone rep puts me on hold for a minute to "look for any deals" and always comes back with something around $6/month for my cars and the app on my tablet/computer. It's annoying to have to do, but it works.

For streaming live tv and recorded shows, use the trial hack discussed above to get it all free for about half the year, and decide which you like best. Try tv.youtube.com, hulu.com, sling.com, atttvnow.com, and the others that pop up. Get a good, high quality HD antenna as a one-time expense that will provide local channels even when the others are down (good for emergencies!).

Phones

Almost every client I've had is paying way, way too much for their cell phones and the service. For the phones, do you really need the very latest model? I always buy one model down on gazelle.com or swappa.com and save a ton on new or like-new phones. While I'm there, I sell my old phones. Please, please don't take a loan on your dang cell phone and bundle that into your payment. Is that worth your freedom?

For service, we use consumercellular.com, pay rock-bottom prices for great service on the AT&T or TMobile networks and the best customer service we've ever had. mint.com is popular, but recently sold (out?) to TMobile. visible.com is the lower-cost service from Verizon and uses their network. ting.com uses the Verizon network as well. Xfinity mobile has good choices for those who use them for internet. Your coverage is no different in these low-cost choices! Verizon, TMobile, and AT&T consistently have the highest prices and worst service. Getting locked into a contract is a thing of the past with others. coveragecritic.com has recent reviews of choices.

If you're not on an unlimited plan, make sure you're connecting to any safe wifi networks whenever you can. Your phone should have a setting to do that.

Medical Costs/Insurance

Check the going rate for medical, dental, vision at sites like health.costhelper.com or opscost.com. Make sure you're not getting ripped off! Use websites like healthgrades.com and webmd.com to check for a highly rated physician. We cover all insurances in Chapter 6.

Be careful about buying your own dental plan, or maybe even signing up for the one at work. Many dental insurance plans are full of holes and exclusions. Talk to your dentist's billing specialist—they know which, if any, are good. Often dentists have their own plans, or will steeply discount services if you don't have insurance. Dental schools typically provide great care for free or low cost. It's common for folks to travel to other countries to get high-quality dental work done for much less, and make a vacation out of it.

If you're over 65 check into aao.org/eyecare-america for free eye care.

If you need health insurance, the go-to these days is healthcare.gov. You can usually click a quickie calculator button to game out a rate anonymously based on your zip code and income. Other choices are COBRA (expensive) and health sharing ministries. Going without health insurance is not a solution. Check healths herpa.com for other options.

There are lots of ways to save on prescriptions. We won't recommend GoodRX, since they just got busted for illegally sharing customer info. Good practices are to always get the generic version of the meds if available, and get them delivered in 90-day supplies via mail order. If there's no generic, see if the drug manufacturer has a rebate on it (go to their web page) and see if it's available on Mark Cuban's costplusdrugs.com. Ask your doctor if there's a clinical trial you can take part in.

Don't forget, there are federal and state programs that forgive hospital/medical debts for families that meet certain criteria. Most hospitals are non-profit and have a requirement to forgive a certain amount of debt each year. Don't talk to the billing folks, ask for the benevolence or forgiveness people. Unpaid medical debt under $500 should no longer appear on your credit report, because of recent legislation.

The absolute best way to save on medical costs is to review and question every charge. It's far too common for the ancient computer systems and overworked, stressed claims people to make mistakes. That claim goes through many people and systems before the bill gets to you. You're probably paying too much!

Pets

I eliminated $60-$100/month grooming costs by getting a top quality Wahl pet grooming kit at Costco. It came with a DVD (videos also on YouTube) that showed how to groom different breeds/sizes of dogs. The first few times, our fur baby was embarrassed to go outside in front of her friends, but I eventually got better at it. It's our bonding time (just kidding, she hates being groomed).

We love Chewy.com for all things pet supplies, especially prescriptions. They're a fraction of what the vet charges! Don't feed your furry family member crappy dog food. It will only come back to bite you (sorry!) in the end when their health becomes poor. Our baby gets FreshPet.

Most pet insurances are overpriced and full of find print/exclusions. The latest ratings I've seen say good things about ASPCA and Healthy Paws, but it's a changing landscape. See if there's a veterinary school nearby that does free or low-cost care as part of training.

Household

Look into places like care.com and sittercity.com for highly vetted, certified child care help. Instead of buying new, check into Goodwill, Salvation Army, and Habitat for Humanity stores for great stuff that's donated from estates. Those stores use their profits to help needy people. Win-win! Frequent yard sales and garage sales for great bargains. Cut your sponges in half to extend their use, use cheaper paper towels instead of embossed paper napkins at dinner time.

Ditch the expensive lawn care, pool care, and other services and learn to do those things yourself, if you are able. Put on a podcast and use that time for learning and exercise in the great outdoors! You can learn to do just about anything with websites like youtube.com, houzz.com, and thisoldhouse.com. Be careful and hire a pro for things like electricity. My wife fired me from plumbing jobs when she went into the bathroom, flushed the toilet, and the shower turned on.

That said, websites like thumbtack.com and handy.com are good places to find someone to take care of things you can't. Don't buy tools for one-time jobs! Go ask a neighbor if they have one you can borrow.

Gifts

Resist the temptation to overdo it. Take care of yourself first, and you can be more generous later. Let friends/family know you're taking a break—they'll probably be relieved they don't have to buy you anything either! Gift more inexpensive sentimental things like finding a nice photo of you and the person and frame it with a nice inscription. Far better than some rando whatever from the big Amazon Prime Days sale! That said, some folks wait until Prime Days to buy all their gifts for the entire year on the cheap. Etsy.com is a great place to get handmade, custom, sentimental gifts (and you're supporting someone else's side hustle!)

Buy those greeting cards at the dollar store for big savings. Or make them yourself. I always throw the store-bought ones I get away, unless someone has taken the time to write something other than "Happy Birthday." I always keep the handmade ones. Who could toss something like that?

Clothing

You probably already have enough in your home to last you, like, forever. C'mon now. Re-use! Growing kids are different. I'm sure your friends and relatives have kids that have outgrown stuff. Don't be afraid to ask them and barter. Second-hand boutiques, yard sales/garage sales, Salvation Army, Goodwill, and online sites like mercari.com and poshmark.com are loaded with new or almost new quality duds at great prices. Why pay top dollar? Sell your stuff there too, while you're at it. You can easily zero out your clothing expense that way.

Travel

Think about using the train rather than the airline if you can. We love the train—no TSA shakedown, easy seating and itinerary changes, bar/dining car, being grounded, and great scenery. They have private cars for extra luxury. Even the better bus lines like Megabus are better than airlines or driving, in my opinion.

If you're flying, try to make your reservations at least 45 days ahead for domestic, 75 days for international trips. Remember, you cancel within 24 hours of booking without a charge! Big box stores like Costco, Sam's Club, BJs have great travel/vacation deals. Pack light and avoid those ridic baggage fees.

When To Buy

Here are the best times of the year to buy certain items, according to Consumer Reports. Some obvious, some not so much!

January: linens and bedding, exercise equipment, winter clothing

February: TVs, tax-filing software, cookware and small kitchen appliances

March: skis and snowboards, high-end fashion, luggage

April: tires, cruise vacations, hotel discounts on tax day

May: mattresses, smart-home hubs, office furniture

June: gardening tools, gym memberships, camping gear

July: swimwear, air conditioners

August: laptops, school supplies, shoes

September: older iPhone models, grills, summer clothing

October: outgoing models of sedans and SUVs, Halloween costumes, patio furniture

November: gaming systems, tablets, large appliances

December: jewelry, toys, wedding dresses

In closing this section, if you don't have time to seek out all the savings on things, there are services that will do some of that for you, and of course, take a cut. One is asktrim.com, but I haven't tried it (I enjoy the chase, myself). Ok, you're all consumer-hacked up and ready to save. We'll cover education and insurance in separate chapters, since they're bigger topics.

"If you buy things you don't need, soon you will have to sell things you do need."

Warren Buffett

Chapter Five

Dealing with Debt

Flip the Script and Take Control

"Never spend your money before you have it."
Thomas Jefferson

First, be aware that most types of debt expire after 3-7 years of *no activity* on your part. It depends on your state. That's why collectors will try to entice you into paying something ridiculously small—$5, for example. Don't fall for it! Doing that resets the clock. If the clock has expired, gently remind the collector of this and ask them to stop contacting you. It can stay on your credit report for up to seven years. Challenge it to the credit reporting bureaus (Equifax, Experian, TransUnion) to get it removed earlier.

Keep in mind that with recent legislation, medical debt under $500 can't be reported on your credit report. See the tips on getting medical debt lowered or dismissed in the previous chapter.

Suppose you stop paying on your HighFee Bank, credit card (or some other unsecured debt—personal loan, medical bills, etc). After a while, the company you owe the money to will decide you will not pay going forward. You're too small for them to chase around and deal with, so they decide instead to take a nice, sweet tax writeoff on your unpaid debt. As a bonus, they'll sell that debt off to a debt collector company for **four cents on the dollar**!

Let's do some simple math. If you owed $10,000 on your card, the debt gets sold to Sleazo Collectors LLC for just $400. Now Sleazo has the full legal right to pursue you for the debt. They will unleash their army of minimum wage script-reading sadist bullies on you. You'll may get phone calls threatening to garnish your wages, ruin your credit score, take your car or house, get you fired, or any manner of horrible outcomes. Imagine you're intimidated into giving them $10,000 for something they paid $400 for—what a huge profit for them! Their costs are low, they don't like to spend money. They leverage fear.

However, we said this was **unsecured** debt. That means there's no property tied to it. A car loan is secured debt—if you don't pay, they come get the car. But credit cards and the type we're discussing are unsecured. They're based only on a promise (by you) to pay them. You are fully within your rights to tell that Sleazo employee on the phone to go pound sand and block the number. They got nuthin'—so far.

What they can do is file a docket with your local court. In most cases, this doesn't happen unless the amount owed is pretty high—tens of thousands. They will not travel from their cave in Sleazo City to get a few bucks from you. They might hire a low-cost local attorney to show up and represent them. That's because if you ignore the court notice and don't show up, they win a judgement by default. That means they now have the power to take action against your wages, or other assets. Ignore nothing that looks like a court notice! It may even be bogus, a carefully crafted letter that looks like a real court notice. Call the court (if it mentions one) and ask if there's an actual filing.

It's scary to receive court notices, but you can take control. I've had clients show up, and the other attorney doesn't, and they dismiss the case. You win, now you owe nothing! I had one client show up, only to be coached on what to say by the rental lawyer representing Sleazo! There are ways to head this off before it ever goes to court. They don't want to go through this expense and hassle. If this happens, it's time to call and try to settle it before the court date. Let them know you're not intimidated by it though, it's a scare tactic in most cases. Don't let it work. If you go to court, you can just refuse to say anything incriminating against yourself or even testify.

The first thing you should do if someone calls you and says you owe money is ask who they are. Don't give them any information yet! They may make it sound like they work for HighFee Bank, but actually be from Sleazo. Sometimes creditors won't sell off the debt, but hire collectors to get the money and pay them a commission. You need to know the difference. Ask them directly if they are doing contract work for HighFee Bank or if they've bought the debt and now own it (and ask for proof). Call HighFee to verify this information before you proceed! They are required to send it **within five days**. Ask them to include the name of the creditor, the amount owed, how you can dispute the debt, and the name and address of the original creditor. If you don't request this within thirty days, you automatically admit the validity of the debt. Do it in writing, so it's documented.

If they've purchased the debt, you have a legal right to demand that they prove to you they now own it. Sometimes, Sleazo is so disorganized they can't even produce the proof. If that's the case, it's case closed. They may have been a scammer all along, just fishing for some personal information or a payment from you. Never assume someone calling you about something like this is legit.

There are rules about how collectors can behave when contacting you. Let them know you're aware of those. Put them on the defensive. A few are below.

- Can't swear, threaten to harm you or your property, can't threaten you with illegal actions, or threaten you with actions they don't intend to take

- Can't make repeated calls over a short period to annoy or harass you. Can't call outside of 8am to 9pm your time, or contact you at work if you tell them not to

- Can't make false or misleading statements

- Can't discuss the matter with anyone but you, your spouse, or your attorney (if you have one)

- Must contact your attorney, not you, if they're aware you have one

That said, now that you understand how all this works, **you have great power**. If the deal is legit, and Sleazo owns the debt, you're in charge. Always communicate and be professional, with a take-charge tone of voice. You are in command. You have all the power. A good opening salvo would be to remind the caller that you're aware they likely bought the debt for pennies on the dollar. Let them know things are tight right now, as evidenced because you missed the payments. It's better to communicate via email than phone, so you have a record of what was discussed. Insist on it.

"Hello! I received the documentation showing you own the debt and verified that with my bank. I understand how the process works, and that you bought my obligation at a highly discounted rate. Things are tough right now. I'm trying to avoid bankruptcy, but if I can scratch together $800, will you consider this debt paid in full and remove it from my credit report? That's a 100% profit for you, after all!"

Notice something important about that tact. You never told them you have the money in hand. That would be a mistake. It gives them leverage. Choose your words carefully. After saying something like that to them, they will probably either laugh or go ballistic. Their job is to collect the entire $10,000 sum—a 2,500% profit! Listen calmly, be courteous, and ask them to email you back if they reconsider. Tell them you're going to move on to the next person you owe money to and see if they want your $800. Spoiler alert: They'll likely email back and accept your offer at some point. It may take several rounds of negotiation. Don't give them power by letting them upset you or becoming emotional. Be strong. Don't feel shame or embarrassment. It's just business. I wouldn't pay over 25-30% of the original balance, in the end. They're usually not allowed to tack on interest and penalties, so don't fall for that. If the debt has been retained by the original creditor (HighFee Bank in this example) and they've just hired the collectors, the best you can typically do is pay half what you owed. In this case, they may be amenable to work-out options, like freezing the account, dropping any penalties and the interest rate, with an agreement that you'll pay it off within a few years. That's a good deal, push for it.

Include this language, and get them to respond that they agree to settle the debt in full upon your payment. That language is very important. You don't want them coming back and saying it was a "payment" toward the balance. You also want them to agree in writing to remove it from your credit report. Never give them your bank account info to withdraw the money! Once they have that, they may take the whole deal. Send them a check, a prepaid debit card, a bank/certified check, or some other secure method of payment. Send by certified mail, signature required.

Note I mentioned the 'b' word there—bankruptcy. That's the last thing they want you to do, because you may well get the debt completely dismissed! It's another tool to put them on the defensive, to make them feel motivated and eager to take whatever they can get. You may even consider bankruptcy. It's not a magic pill and is often a bad move. There are two types of consumer bankruptcy—Chapter 7 and Chapter 13. Chapter 7 is the magic one, where some debts may get wiped off the slate (but not secured debt, IRS/tax, or student loans). But you're unlikely to qualify for that if you have a job or other assets like lots of equity in your home. Things have to be terrible to get that, and you'll have to pay thousands to a lawyer and wear that stain for the rest of your life. Sure, it will come off your credit report in 7-10 years, but there's always that question on job and other applications—"Have you **ever** filed for bankruptcy?"

You're likely to get Chapter 13, which basically just sets up a repayment plan to pay off the debt, plus the thousands owed to an attorney. You can do that yourself on the cheap, without the stain, just by following the advice in this book!

After the deal is done, don't forget to keep checking your credit report to ensure the debt is gone. Give it some time, and if you're not getting success, then challenge the item by providing the proof that the creditor agreed that it's paid in full and that they'd remove it. Also, remember forgiven debt is taxable as income. You will receive a 1099 form to file with your taxes. That part sucks, but it's a still a huge win if you got $9,200 of debt forgiven! Bear it in mind and save up to pay the taxes, so you don't end up back in the hole at tax time.

If you've had a vehicle or other property repossessed, remember it's sold at auction and you only owe the difference between what you owed and what they received at auction. Don't be confused into paying the entire sum you owed!

> *"Debt is like any other trap, easy enough to get into, but hard enough to get out of."*
>
> Josh Billings

CHAPTER SIX

Insurances

(BOOORING?)

"Fun is like life insurance; the older you get, the more it costs."

Frank McKinney Hubbard

Nobody wants to think about insurance. It's pretty boring stuff, right? True, but it's also the "sleep well at night" stuff—as long as you're not getting ripped off by the wrong kind. Sometimes, especially with your finances, boring is good. If you want excitement, find a roller coaster. Most people are paying way too much for insurance, or don't have good coverage. Maybe all the above! It's no coincidence that it's the names of big insurance companies on those huge sports stadiums.

But wouldn't it suck to use the knowledge in this book to become financially independent and wealthy, only to have it all wiped out because your insurance wasn't right? That's why this chapter is essential. I've seen people brag about their low premiums for auto or other types of insurance. That can be a huge red flag. Maybe it means their coverage stinks, and you don't find that out until something terrible happens. Attorneys are always looking for someone to sue, and that's typically where your insurance comes in. You know what? Like everything else, when it's done right, it's not complicated. If you don't understand it, something is wrong. I've seen years of hard work and mountains of wealth wiped out just because the insurances were wrong or nonexistent.

And listen, if you think you don't need health insurance because you're young and healthy, or don't need auto insurance because you drive carefully and stay close to home, you're just tempting fate and acting foolish. This will probably hurt you in a major way at some point. Karma is a you-know-what. Don't tempt it.

Let's cover each type.

Life Insurance

Repeat after me: *Life insurance is for someone who depends on your income, should the worst happen to you.* There are two broad categories of life insurance.

Term Life Insurance. This is a simple (we like simple!) agreement between you and the insurance company. You pay them a (typically) low, inexpensive payment each month for an agreed-upon number of years, and if you die during that time, they will pay your beneficiary (or beneficiaries) the agreed amount of money. Easy-peasy! Suppose you've done the math, read this book, and know that in ten years you'll be financially independent and your kids will be out of college. You don't need life insurance after that. It's a waste of money.

Cash-Value/Permanent/Whole Life Insurance. When they say "permanent" and "whole" life, they ain't kidding. With these, you're agreeing to pay **for the rest of your life**! Why would you sign up for that when you're on track to be wealthy and self-funded at a pretty young age? Who depends on your income at age 70? 80? 90? What if the insurance company goes bust or sells your policy to some sketchy off-shore outfit? It's gonna stink making those payments at that age. Oh, wait, they'll tell you it's an investment, or a savings & loan account. Bull. We'll get to that.

How much do you need and for what? Review the list below and do a little math. That's your number.

- Final burial expenses (if you don't already have enough cash for that)

- Readjustment time for spouse/partner (if work doesn't pay for it)

- Income replacement (stay-at-home spouses/partners have value!)

- Debt repayment (maybe pay the house off...)

- Education expenses for kiddos

Based on the above, it should be clear that you don't need to take out life insurance policies for your dependent kids, unless you don't have the money for burial expenses. Toss those guilt-tripping Gerber mail circulars and emails. If your spouse/partner stays at home and something happens to them, remember you're now probably going to hire someone to do those things. Also note that the above list doesn't include "leave my heirs a legacy." No. You do that by being financially responsible, building actual wealth, and maybe leaving behind a paid-for house as well.

If you have medical problems and can't get term life coverage, consider mortgage insurance or adding extra group coverage through your employer at open enrollment. Those don't require a physical. You don't want to rely on employer insurance alone, because if you get laid off, you might find yourself without insurance. They usually give you an offer to buy it if you separate from the company.

Let's get back to that "other" kind. There are many varieties of permanent life insurance. You might hear it referred to as whole life, universal, indexed, variable, fixed-index, maximum premium indexing (MPI), or whatever the latest catchy, confusing name is that they try to label it. It's lipstick on the same ole' pig. This kind of complex life insurance costs around 5-8 times what term does.

They'll tell you it's an investment, but the policies typically cap returns on your end of the deal. So, if the S&P 500 takes off on a 30% gain like it has in a few recent years, you might get only 8% (or less) of that. Guess who gets the rest? They'll tell you they'll let you borrow from it. Yeah, you can also do that without asking anyone if you just get inexpensive term and bank or invest the difference! It's perilous. As with other insurance products, like annuities, if the insurance company goes out of business (or sells your policy to another that does), you are outta luck. Get in line with others in the bankruptcy creditor line or your state bailout fund (if there is one) and good luck. Some insurance companies go out of business. Nobody dreamed a biggie like Washington Mutual would. There is no FDIC (savings account) or SPIC (investing accounts) insurance on these. Kinda ironic, isn't it? Simple wins. We like simple, inexpensive, manageable, understandable, non-risk. These products are none of those. They are a big fat blob cloud of uncertainty and make precise planning difficult. Don't believe me? Try to pin your insurance salesperson down on exactly how much you'll get and when. Ask them to guarantee it in writing, and show you *all* of your *exact* fees over the years in writing, including commissions, M&E fees, fund fees, wrap fees, admin fees, management fees, on and on.

Look, we know diversification is important. Diversification wins. You wouldn't take a big chunk (or all) of your nest egg and invest it in a single company's stock, right? (Right?). We'll talk about how ridiculous and risky that is in the chapters on investing. Most people know it's crazy. I don't care if you love the company. You don't know what's going on behind the scenes there or at their competitors. Enron. Kodak. The list of "sure things" that went bust goes on. So why would you take a big pile of your hard-earned money and hand it over (yes, you are buying a product, so it's gone) to a *single* insurance company that could go bankrupt, or sell your product off to another that could go bankrupt? It's the opposite of diversification. No, it's not "guaranteed income." It's not insured. Yeah, there are state bailout funds. Good luck with that. Some are pennies on the dollar, and some cap at very low coverage. People feel safe by buying policies from well-known companies (the ones with their names on all those sports stadiums) but then get sold down the river when their policy is farmed off to some risky off-shore company they never heard of.

The other thing is, people assume that if the face value is say, $250,000, and they build their savings/investment account up to say, $200,000, their heirs will get $450,000 if they die. But no—$200,000 of the $250,000 payout comes from your savings, and the insurance company is only on the hook for $50,000. Huh?

Insurance products (life insurance, annuities) are one time where it's **essential** to actually read the contract. If you can't understand it, run. Run fast and far. For life insurance, there's a common expression, "Buy term and invest the rest." I fully believe in that! We'll cover how to invest later in this book.

Where to buy? Many of the online sites that claim to find the best deal are just fronts for the big insurance companies. Or, they exist to capture your personal info and sell it to them, resulting in you getting bombarded with emails and phone calls. I use and like zanderins.com, who I've found to get us the best deals and keep our info private. If you walk into a 'captive' agency such as State Farm or Allstate brick and mortar store, they'll only sell you their brand. If you go to a local brick and mortar insurance broker, they're a middle person, and you'll pay more than just going somewhere like Zander or directly online to the big companies like Progressive or GEICO.

Auto Insurance

Are you in good hands? Let's find out. They typically break auto insurance out into sections. Let's cover them.

Liability. This covers you when you're responsible for an accident that causes losses to others. There are usually three liability sections/coverages. The first one is the max your insurance company will pay out to cover medical expenses for a single person in the other car. Next is what they will pay out (max) for multiple injured people. The third number is what they'll pay for property damage (you run down someone's mailbox or smash into their garage, for example). So, if you see something like 25/50/30 that means your insurance company will pay out max $25,000 to one person, $50,000 max for multiple people, and $30,000 to repair that property you damaged. When you consider an ambulance ride alone can max that out (let alone a $40k life-flight helicopter ride!), that's pretty crappy coverage. What happens if someone has $200,000 in medical costs and your insurance company hands them a check for $50,000? Right. They sue you. Not good. At a minimum, you want 100/300/50.

Medical Payments/Personal Injury Protection (PIP). This is coverage of medical expenses for you and your passengers. In some states, you can opt out of this is you have great health insurance already (called health care primary option). But don't do that unless you've run it by your health insurance company (they may not allow it). It's not recommended to drop PIP!

Uninsured/Underinsured. What if someone causes an accident, hurts you, and they don't have insurance? It's not that uncommon. In that case, you're stuck—unless you have this coverage. So, don't drop it! There are more uninsured, broke, drunk, knuckleheads out there texting their baby mamas and watching YouTube while driving than you'd like to think. Protect yourself. The coverages here can be 'stacked,' meaning you can take the amount spread across multiple vehicles on your policy and apply it to one incident, if it's a biggie.

Vehicle Damage. Now we get to your buggy. This part covers getting your ride fixed. Many states have no-fault coverage, which means if there's a "situation," your own insurance covers your car, no matter who caused the problem. This is the section that most people think about when they think about auto insurance. This is where your deductibles come into play. If you have a $250 deductible, you pay the first $250 of repairs, and the insurance company picks up the rest. There are two parts to this—collision and comprehensive. Collision covers the damage due to a (duh) collision. Comprehensive covers non-collision stuff like hail damage, rocks hitting your car on the road, trees falling on it while parked, and collisions with non-car objects like deer. These are optional unless you have a lien/loan/lease on the car. If your vehicle is a beater that you wouldn't bother getting fixed, factor that into your coverage decision. I'd keep it, because if it's totaled, you'd want enough to get another beater. Save some money on your premiums and boost your deductible to $500-$1,000 (you have at least $1,000 in your emergency fund, right?).

Full Tort vs Limited Tort. This can be confusing. It's related to your ability to sue. If you're hit and experience medical expenses and/or lost wages, those are easy to prove and recover a damage settlement for. What if you've also been traumatized, and experienced less provable, tangible problems like stress, PTSD, quality of life? If you have full tort, your insurance company will help with the legal expenses for the latter. Otherwise, you're on your own for that part. But, keep in mind, if it's an obvious case of negligence on the other driver, you'll have attorneys lined up to represent you free up front, for a percentage of the settlement.

Other ways to get your rates down:

- Got kids on the policy? Students with B average get better rates

- Assign the lowest-value car to the person who drives the most miles

- Lower your rate by taking online classes, and being a safe driver!

- Ask about any group/association discounts

- Ask about Health Care Primary option to lower your personal injury protection (PIP)

- Bundling with homeowners, umbrella, renters is good

- Monitoring gadgets - intrusion, privacy, usually not in your favor

- Use zanderins.com to check rates

- Check directly with discount insurers (Progressive, GEICO) rather than through an agent

- USAA may cost a bit more, but it consistently rates high

Check your policy carefully. Are you paying for unnecessary add-ons? For example, are you paying for roadside/towing coverage when you're already paying for AAA? Are you paying for rental car coverage while your car is in the shop when you already have a backup vehicle?

Health Insurance

Employers cover most everyone, but these days with copays, coinsurance, deductibles, you've still got plenty of skin in the game. The choices presented to you during annual benefits enrollment, open enrollment if you're pursuing the Affordable Care

Act (ACA/Obamacare), or Medicare enrollment can be daunting. High-deductible plans can be costly if you have health problems, but a bonus if you're pretty healthy—especially when you factor in the sweet Health Savings Account (HSA) they usually include. Most sites have calculators that will ask you what preexisting conditions you have, how many doctor visits you have per year, etc and provide some guidance on which plan options are best. Sites like healthsherpa.com can also guide you through options.

Back in the olden times, health care was the biggest thing holding people back from retiring before age 65, when they become eligible for Medicare. The ACA has made early retirement possible by providing subsidized, inexpensive health care to anyone who doesn't have employer-based or other options. If you're pursuing FIRE, it's important to go on healthcare.gov or your state portal and use the quickie calculator to find out what your cost may be in early retirement. Too many people don't factor that cost in, and hence they fail at FIRE. That said, some living the FIRE lifestyle choose to do so in other countries, where quality healthcare is inexpensive or free.

HSAs are the only way to put money away without paying taxes ever. The amounts you contribute to the fund each year come off your taxable income, it grows tax free, and you don't get taxed when you pull the money out and use it (as long as it's for qualified expenses). The list of things you can spend it on grows considerably after you turn 65. It's a FIRE hack to fund these up and use them for healthcare expenses if/when early retired.

If none of the above are options for you, health sharing plans like sedara.com and chministries.org are options. You can review dental plans at dentalplans.com, but most aren't that great, compared to using the non-insurance rate at your dentist, or taking part in their own in-house plans. Ask their billing specialist for opinions.

Same with vision coverage, although if you're over 65 and have low-income or assets, you may qualify for free exams at aao.org.

Refer to some tips in the prior chapter on savings hacks for more ways to save on health care.

Homeowners/Renters Insurance

Above all, make sure the contents coverage is correct here. What would it cost you to replace your belongings if God forbid there was a fire, flood, burglary, etc? Take photos or videos of your high-value possessions and make sure they're stored on a cloud drive, along with receipts, for quick payment. Don't pay for $300,000 contents coverage if you've only got $50,000 worth of stuff.

For homeowners, make sure it's guaranteed replacement cost, not actual cost coverage. If your house burns, you want to build a similar house at today's prices!

Disability Insurance

This coverage will replace lost income because of a short-term or long-term disability. It's more important for folks with physical jobs than desk jockeys, but everyone should have it if you're working. COVID took a lot of office workers off the job, and long COVID is a real thing, affecting cognitive abilities. Buy the kind that affects your particular kind of work (called occupational or own-occupation coverage). Normally you have some level of short-term coverage through work, but check to be sure. That, plus a 3-6 month emergency fund, is your foundation.

You might consider long-term policies of five years or more. They usually have an "elimination period" which is the time between your disabling incident and when they kick in. So, if you have three months of short-term disability coverage, a 90-day elimination period would be about right. These policies should be non-cancelable (by the insurer) and should cost around 1-3% of your income per year. Your employer may supply it as a benefit, or it might be an optional add-on during benefits open enrollment period. The payout coverage should be around 60-70% of your salary (since if you need this, you probably won't be water skiing or mountain climbing).

Long-Term Care Insurance

This is coverage for nursing home care, or in-home care when you aren't able to do the basic life functions anymore, or there's nobody to help you with them. We're talking about things like dressing, bathing, toileting, feeding yourself. People in my family tend to keel over from heart attacks, so we're not great candidates for long-term care coverage. Examine your family lineage when making this decision. My mom is in her late 80s and still living alone, taking care of business. My wife's mom is in her mid-90s and still living alone and taking care of herself! It's said the sweet spot for signing up for this type of coverage is right about when you turn 60. Does your family have a legacy of taking care of their own elderly members? If so, and the younger generations are on board, you may not need as much or any. I recommend having a plan for this. The worst case is, if you've saved the money and your kids take care of you, you can leave it to them as your thanks.

Back in the day, folks started shuttling off their assets to their kids or other family members "to hold" so that they could look broke enough to get free nursing home care from Medicaid. Don't do that. This isn't the 1950s. All your financial transactions are subject to the algorithms that sniff out this kind of behavior. You don't want your old-timers home to have bars. Maybe the kind with pina coladas, but not the kind with iron ones!

Statistically, by the time people need this kind of help, they only need it for 2-3 years. So, if you're going to purchase it, don't get sold on some crazy-long benefit by an overzealous insurance agent fishing for a big commission. Anyway, if you're following the advice in this book, you should be self-funded (again, the best and cheapest kind of insurance!) by the time you need it. When we get to talking about retirement planning, you want to factor this cost in. genworth.com has a pretty good anonymous calculator, so use that to get an idea of future costs.

The problems I have with long-term care insurance are related to other "future" types of insurance like whole life/cash value and annuities. You're taking a risk that the insurance company will still be around when you need the money. The policies often have an "elimination" period, which means on the day you need it, you may have to wait days, weeks, or months before they kick in their share. Of course, they're hoping you're in such terrible shape that you "eliminate" in the interim. They're off the hook, and keep 100% of your donations, er, premiums. LTC policies often won't cover or have very limited coverage for the most likely reason you'll need them—alzheimers/dementia. That's a show-stopper for me as well. They might not even cover the type of assisted living facility you've chosen.

Case Study: I spoke to a new client today who was quite concerned about this. Her mother had gone into a long-term care facility, but her policy had a 90-day elimination period. Her mom passed away halfway through that. It was a heart-breaking story, not only losing her mom but having to foot the bill even after being diligent enough to sign up for coverage and paying those premiums for so long. The new client and I built that self-funded cost into her financial plan.

Self-fund when at all possible! Use that Genworth calculator. At this writing, the cost of assisting living is around an average of $4,500/month. Nursing home rooms are between $7,800 and $8.700 depending on whether you want private or semi-private. Home health aids are around $27/hour. Keep in mind some areas of the country have much higher costs of living than others.

If you get talked into getting a long-term care rider on a whole life insurance policy, you lose the ability to itemize that deduction as a medical cost. Often, when we get to that late stage in life, our medical/long-term care costs are so high and our taxable income is so low, we can finally take advantage of itemizing our deductions. Don't throw that opportunity away!

We talk about LTC a bit more in the chapter on Social Security and Medicare.

Umbrella Insurance

Now we get to the good stuff, the best kind! Remember waaay back in the auto insurance section when I told you that $50,000 personal liability was dangerous because someone could have $200,000 of medical costs in an accident you cause, and sue you? Then I said that $100,000 was a good amount to have? That made little sense, did it? You'd still be on the hook for the extra $100,000! That's where umbrella insurance comes in. It's the magical umbrella over all your other insurances and it picks up where they leave off. If someone gets hurt in your house, on your boat or jet ski, your vehicle insurance pays their part, then the umbrella company steps in to cover the rest. It's typical to have policies of $500,000, one million, or more. It's pretty inexpensive—and great sleep well at night stuff.

You'll often hear that you don't need this if you don't have a big net worth or a lot of assets. Bunk. You might not now, but if someone sues you and is awarded a judgement, they'll track you until the end of your days, and pounce the minute they smell money around you. It's a best practice to bundle this with your auto, homeowners/renters, and other insurances to make sure everything fits together nicely, and there are no gaps in coverage.

Annuities

As we'll discuss later, people get scared and intimidated by anything to do with investing. They've heard dramatic, exaggerated tales of others who have lost it all. Usually, that's because they broke some rules we'll talk about in the chapters on investing. This is where the insurance salespeople swoop in, to leverage that fear and uncertainty. "We'll take all the risk for you! Guaranteed income!" they'll whisper in your ear, often over a "free" steak dinner with a room full of other potential marks.

Here's the concept of an annuity. You take your nest egg, that (hopefully) big pile of money you worked so hard to save up, and hand it over to the insurance company. That's right, they're not investing it for you, as would happen if you allowed an investment advisor to manage it for you (don't do that either). You are actually buying a "product." Your money is gone, in return for a promise by the insurance company to make regular payments to you, either immediately or in the future. There will be no leaving it behind to your cherubs unless you buy an expensive death benefit rider. The insurance company invests your money, makes bank, and in return gives you savings account levels of return. Not such a good deal. We'll teach you how to cut out the middle person and invest it yourself.

Remember when we said earlier that diversification always wins over the long haul? That diversification is important? In the investing chapter, we'll talk about why it's dangerous to invest in individual companies. So, knowing all that, why would you take your entire nest egg and give it to one company? Put all those eggs in one basket? Because the problem is that if the insurance company goes belly-up, or sells your annuity off to another company that goes belly-up, you're kind of screwed. There's no FDIC (savings) or SIPC (investing) type of insurance on insurance products like whole life or annuities. How ironic!

If that happens, you get in line with all the other bankruptcy creditors and hope to get paid something. Different states have some form of bailout fund or program, but some are quite meager. In NJ, for example, they limit your loss recovery to $100k, and that's if the money is in the fund and at the state's discretion. To get a meaningful annuity payment, you'd have to fork over much more than $100k. I just read a Wall Street Journal article about a guy who made himself a billionaire by selling billions of dollars in annuities to thousands of people, who now have no access to the money because of his corruption. Because he refuses to go bankrupt, they can't even get any state bailout money.

These payments aren't indexed for inflation. The $1,000/month you get might sound great right now, but in the not too distant future, that might seem like a tiny amount of money, with inflation. The contracts are very complex, full of loopholes that benefit the insurance company, and the fees are egregious and very hard to track. They're commission driven, which explains the "free" steak dinners and fast-talking salespeople. As well, some states that don't tax your Social Security, pension, or IRA distributions may tax your annuity distributions.

Deferred (the kind that start paying you later) annuities have gone through a list of fancy renaming over the years, as the old name was associated with problems and they needed fresh lipstick on the pig, just like we discussed with their cousin products, whole life insurance, above. Reps will tell you the newer kind allow you to invest, and you can pick your investments. That's great, except for the language in the contracts that cap your returns at single digits when the market is returning great double digits, and again, that's net of fees.

Some investment advisors will even talk people into buying annuities (or moving existing ones) and putting them in their IRAs! Now you're not only paying the egregious hidden fees inside the annuities, you're paying your advisor their 1% or more on top of that. To me, that's pure evil. Now they're talking about giving the insurance companies an enormous gift by allowing annuities to be a choice in employer-sponsored plans like 401ks. The lobbyists are hard at work in DC.

Do annuities ever make sense? Let's return to one of our founding principles in this book—simple is better. Suppose you're sitting there at 82 years old, no longer wishing to rely on the stock market. The stock market is for the long haul, and there isn't really a long haul left. Your cognitive abilities may be diminishing. If you've got significant assets at this point, given these factors, it's not crazy to take a chunk and buy the *simplest* form of annuity, a single-premium immediate annuity (SPIA) late in life, multi-year guaranteed annuity (MYGA, often also used to bridge the gap until collecting Social Security), or QLAC (discussed in the retirement chapter). These are the equivalent of level term life insurance, a simple transaction and agreement. You turn over a pile of money, and the insurance company begins immediate monthly payments to you, for the rest of your life or the term.

However, you still have some of the above risks. They could go out of business, sell your annuity off-shore, and you can no longer leave that money behind to your heirs or charity. It's gone. If you have three million, it's not the end of the world to take $600k and do something like this. I'm more a fan of building your own annuity with safe, simple US treasury bonds (or funds), or maybe laddering those and/or some simple certificates of deposit. Then, the money is still yours. It's safe, and you can leave it behind. Some suggest the immediate annuity route in examples like this, where you're just using a portion of your assets. You still have the same problems with the rest of it, the bulk of it—you have to figure out where to put it. So, it doesn't really solve that problem. Vanguard exited the annuity business long ago.

I'll say it again, and often. ***The fewer people and rules between you and your money, the better.***

Case Study: I had a client that had been talked into one of these products. She wanted it to pay her when she turned 55, her intended retirement age. I read through her contract and had to inform her the policy was written differently. They had tacked on her spouse, who is ten years younger, and made the annuity payments start when *he* turned 55, ten years after she needed the money. She cried, I cried, then we both got mad, and wrestled that money back to invest.

Case Study: A client was sold an annuity while going through a very difficult divorce and getting her taxes done. She was in a vulnerable state, nobody to run it by at the time, and believed it was a safe thing to do because the company was Prudential, "The Rock," a company that's been around for around a hundred and fifty years. She trusted that name and reputation. Trust the Rock, right? In the United States, insurance companies are required by law to keep big cash reserves to ensure they can make those payments. They are also required to adopt stringent accounting practices and regulatory oversight and compliance. That's pretty reassuring! Well, this client received a letter that Prudential had sold her annuity to some off-shore company based in Bermuda.

Guess what? All those reassuring laws and regulations are gone. The new company is free to play fast and loose with the money. They can pay their execs exorbitant salaries for a few years, then, whoops, just declare bankruptcy. They actually hired Prudential as their 3rd party administrator, so the statements and letters still come from "Prudential," which is pretty shady and deceptive.

Professional Liability Insurance

This insurance (also called or related to malpractice or errors & omissions) protects individuals & organizations that provide professional services that are subject to risk, such as doctors or investment advisors. The policy limits, deductibles, and premiums vary based on the profession and level of risk, as well as potential lawsuit amounts. That means it's low for therapists, high for surgeons. It may be required by law in some states, so make sure to get it if at all in doubt. It's usually pretty inexpensive, unless you're a surgeon.

More Insurances to Avoid

- Credit life and disability (credit cards, other loans)

- Cancer and hospital indemnity

- Accidental death and dismemberment (ouch!)

- Prepaid burial expenses (pre-planning is good!)

- Mortgage life insurance (unless you can't get term)

- Policies with fancy options: return of premium, waiver of premium

Other Insurance Topics

These may be considered legal topics, but they're also really insurance against other bad financial things that can happen to you.

Prenuptial Agreements. Prenuptial agreements come up often. If you're both young and have about the same financial status (including your parents), it's not as important as where there's a vast difference. It can be a tough topic and discussion, but it's not for one person to screw the other over and leave them high and dry. The enormous benefit of going through this practice, even if it's an informal, signed and notarized agreement, is to make sure you are both on the same page regarding these plans and decisions. That can save the type of arguments later that end otherwise wonderful relationships. Prenups are very important for people who have children from prior marriages or relationships.

Trusts and Wills. Are your wills in order, including the other related documents like your living will and health care proxy? If not, try Quicken Willmaker or Mama Bear Legal Forms for simple scenarios. You can do most or all of the work yourself, in the privacy of your home, and then get it notarized. Store copies in a safe place, and maybe give copies to your family. You can go the local attorney route, but it will be expensive. If you have complex scenarios, it's well worth the extra cost. I've been using a great in-between solution with clients, trustandwill.com.

Do you need a trust? A trust is for protection and/or control. The best example is leaving money to someone who is underaged.

Use a trust for that and appoint a good trustee to make those decisions. Make sure that trustee is aware and on board with the decision. Make sure they know the criteria under which you want the money dispensed. Other examples of when to leave money in a trust would be for someone who might be irresponsible with money, have addictions or other problems, or a child that has a likelihood of being sued, such as a surgeon. Money in trusts is better protected from lawsuits than more direct assets like brokerage or bank accounts.

Making a trust the beneficiary on your accounts or policies can complicate tax matters, so only do so when you're sure they're needed.

Identity Theft Protection. This is often another over-hyped product that takes advantage of fear. Many of the over-priced name brand services will give you a blob of complicated software that will gum up your devices and slow them down measurably. You can do most of the essential protection tasks on your own by freezing your credit at Experian, Equifax, and TransUnion, never clicking on links in emails, social media, or text messages, keeping your devices up to date with the latest updates, use the great built-in tools, and using contactless methods with your cards instead of swiping/inserting.

I'm averse to putting links or phone numbers in this book, but it's important in this case. Freeze your credit now! It's free and easy to freeze/unfreeze when you need to.

Equifax 866-478-0027 equifax.com/personal/credit-report-ser vices/credit-freeze

TransUnion 888-909-8872 transunion.com/credit-freeze

Experian 888-397-3742 experian.com/freeze/center.html

Be on guard and suspicious of any request to change your password, divulge your last 4 of SSN, driver's license, birth date or other sensitive info. Ask if there's another way to verify who you are. Use two-factor authentication everywhere you can, but absolutely for your money accounts. That's the one where they send you a text code when you attempt to log in. You can tell the systems to remember your primary devices so you don't have to do it all the time. Use a password vault such as the free pwsafe.org (it stores your passwords locally and not off in the cloud somewhere).

Add your phone numbers to the Do Not Call registry at donotcall.gov. Sign up at optoutprescreen.com and catalogchoice.org to eliminate credit card offers and junk mail.

The IRS, Social Security, Medicare, and other government agencies rarely just call out of the blue, so be wary of anyone saying that's who they are on the phone.

All that said, Zander has very reasonable identity theft services at zanderins.com.

Alrighty, gang. You know the basics of insurance now. Get your policies out and review them! Don't let an unexpected event undo all your hard work toward financial independence and building wealth.

CHAPTER SEVEN

Buying and Selling Properties

SAVE THOUSANDS!

"Buy land, they're not making it anymore."
Mark Twain

Remember back at the beginning of this book, when we told you each chapter could be a book on its own? Well, this one actually is. I've written a book on buying and selling homes, now in its second edition. The title is *Show and Sell 2023: Selling Your Home Today, A Cautionary Tale* (it's at Amazon, B&N, and other book outlets). It's mainly about selling, but also has a chapter and tips for buyers. As a buyer, knowing seller tricks and hacks is useful to you as well! It's also full of strange, and lighthearted tales of the adventures I've had selling several homes on my own. One old guy came by my open house just to drink up my beer, and I have to admit, it was a pretty cool hustle. It has tempted me to take it up—safer and easier than wedding crashing. If you're a house flipper, you need this knowledge for sure! But even everyday homeowners can save a ridiculous amount of money when selling their home. Let's cover the basics in this chapter.

Buying a Home

Buy vs Rent

A home is certainly an investment—a big one! Maybe. That concept really began back in the old days, when young families would buy a home and live in it for decades, if not forever. A forever home. That means paying closing costs once, moving costs once. Back then, home value appreciation was pretty much straight-line, up and up. Homeowners also got a much better tax deduction for mortgage interest. In circumstances like that, owning a home was certainly an easier decision.

How much of that really happens in these modern times? Not much. We're much more mobile. People often sell and buy again in less than ten years. That means paying those hefty closing and moving costs, plus associated costs such as improvements and new furniture repeatedly. Do the math. Plenty of analyses find that renting vs owning is a break-even proposition when all things are factored in, given the rate of selling and moving we see out there. Don't think you're buying your 'forever' home. It's very unlikely. You may get transferred at work, have to move for a new job, or sadly, divorced. Your family may need help and cause you to move. Extreme weather plays an increasing factor in forced relocation.

The mortgage interest deduction is no longer a benefit for most people, because you have to itemize and the amounts are capped. Home appreciation isn't the sure thing it once was, as many people learned in the financial crisis of 2008-2009, when home values plummeted and many abandoned their homes, suddenly underwater on their mortgages. More and more homes are being wiped off the map by extreme weather. Communities like the one where the toxic train derailment in East Palestine, Ohio, saw their property values zeroed out in an instant.

The point is, don't rush to buy a house because you're being told you're throwing money away by renting. It's bull. Buying the wrong house, or buying before you're ready, is certainly a good example of throwing money away, and a recipe for financial and domestic stress. If you factor in the expenses associated with owning, there's not a big difference. Examples are mortgage interest, property taxes, bigger utility costs because of the larger space, big-ticket costs such as replacing a HVAC system or roof, more expensive homeowners/private mortgage (PMI) insurance, all the stuff needed to maintain the property, and homeowner association fees. Factor in the extra time and reduced stress of not having to shovel, mow, and rake leaves. You might have access to free resources in your rental community, such as a gym, pool, and clubhouse for parties that you'd have to drive to and pay for when owning a home.

There are plenty of buy vs rent calculators that are an internet search away. The New York Times has a great one—it factors in all the actual costs of home ownership. Be careful and consider the source. Guess which way a calculator that is sponsored by someone who provides mortgages might try to sway you? Hopefully, this section has given you food for thought regarding the decision to buy a home. I'm not against home ownership. I'm for owning the *right* home at the *right* time in your life, with the **right** preparation and an awareness of what can go **wrong** and what can go **right**! It can be a great inflation hedge and essentially a forced savings plan. That's what the section following this one is all about.

Curse or Blessing?

You want the latter, not the former, right? Here are a few simple tips to make sure your new home is a joy.

- Buy with no other debt

- Have the closing costs and a solid emergency fund in place

    ○ Murphy will move in with you

- Buy with at least 10% down (1st home), 20% for later homes

    ○ 20% down avoids paying private mortgage insurance for the bank, paid for by you!

- Monthly payment should be less than 25% of your *take-home* income

    ○ Use NerdWallet or Ally 'how much house can I afford' tools

- Find and use a great home inspector—very important!

    ○ Usually former builders are good

- Always get a survey and title insurance

- Take the sale price and divide it by the square footage to get the cost per square foot

- Look for nearby homes for sale that have a list price below market value

Think hard about that first bullet—having the money on hand for the many expenses you will incur. Not planning for these causes many new homeowners to hit their credit cards hard, which results in a downward financial spiral and stress. Make sure you've thought about the below list and have the cash on hand to tackle any that may even remotely come onto your radar. Be honest with yourself! A good estimate is to set aside 1-2% of home value each year for expenses. Divide it by 12 and put it away each month in your budget.

- Homeowner's Association (HOA) fees

- Property/School Taxes, Homeowner's Insurance, PMI (probably in escrow w/mortgage)

- Furniture/Fixtures

- Repairs (fewer if you hired a very good home inspector)

- Window treatments (if previous homeowner didn't leave them, or they're unsightly)

- Carpets, paint—can you do it yourself to save lots of money?

- HVAC and any appliances the previous owner didn't leave behind or that may be older

- Yard upkeep/snow removal equipment/services, generator, gutter/driveway upkeep

- Higher utility bills because of more square footage

- Monitor that roof. It's an enormous cost to fix/replace, especially if it leaks inside

Strategic Advice

Here are some buying tips. First, don't buy the nicest house on the block. Others will just drag your property value down. Buy in the bottom to middle range of the neighborhood for the best value bang for the buck. Location is key, as they say. Learn all about the area, especially crime rates, the schools, area amenities, etc. If you homeschool or don't have kids, you may think you're doing a hack by getting a great deal in a location where the schools are bad. But when you go to sell, you've eliminated a sizeable group of potential buyers—people with kids. There are websites like areavibes.com, bestplaces.net, city-data.com, and livability.com that allow you to find this information and rank your own specific criteria and find the best suited locations for you. The best hack is to visit the neighborhood on a weekend or just after work, park the car, get out, and chat up the locals. They may have the inside scoop for you—such as a chicken processing plant is going in across the street (pew!).

When you're looking at homes, don't discount ones that have flaws that can be fixed fairly easily with painting or landscaping, for example. Eliminate homes that have problems that are hard to fix, such as bad curb appeal or floor plan. Don't get too excited if the seller offers you a home warranty—many aren't worth the paper they're written on. They can be full of exclusions. If it's a seller's market and very competitive, you can put yourself at the head of the list by being pre-approved (which is better than pre-qualified) or buying with cash. Don't jump the gun when you find 'the one,' rather make several trips. You'll pick up on things you missed the first time through. Take pictures.

Banks usually want a credit score of 720 or above to give you a mortgage. Not having other debt is a very positive factor in your favor, and having paid down that debt will have increased your score. Don't close the accounts, as one of the big factors in your credit score is the amount of available but unused credit. Closing accounts will make this percentage smaller. One hack that many credit score repair companies use is to challenge anything negative on your credit reports shortly before applying for mortgages. This removes them from the report for a period, so that you can prove they are incorrect. During that period, your score goes up. If you don't successfully challenge, they reappear and your score goes back down, but maybe by then you have secured your mortgage.

Services like Experian Boost can help your score by giving credit for on-time rent, utility, and other payments. Make sure you are paying everything on time in the time leading up to your home purchase. That's another big factor in your credit score. Don't open new accounts! That makes the credit agencies nervous and hurts your score. In the end, if your score isn't ideal, it's not the end of the world. Your mortgage rate might be a half-point or so higher. You can also choose a bank that does manual underwriting, which gives you a chance to lobby for your specific circumstances (such as, you haven't had debt in so long you have no credit score, in which case you're my new hero!)

When mortgage shopping, use sites like bankrate.com. FHA and VA loans might or might not be the best. They can accommodate certain groups, but sometimes have high fees. VA loans are great for disabled vets, because they waive the fees. Some will allow you to buy with no down payment. Is that really a good idea? Are you really ready to buy a home if you have nothing saved? You might consider a 15-year vs 30-year mortgage. I'm more in favor of the shorter term, which locks in a lower interest rate and locks you into paying it off earlier. That said, there's no mathematical difference by going with a 30-year and doubling up on the payments. Do you have the discipline to do that?

Closing costs can be anywhere between 2-7% of the loan for buyers. Don't fold them into the loan unless you have a super-low mortgage rate, or even then. Be careful—when you're buying a home, the sharks will be circling. The involved parties know you will be overwhelmed, stressed, and excited during closing and may not read everything carefully. Many of the items on the settlement statement at closing are actually optional or negotiable. Get an early copy and go over it with a fine-tooth comb.

Be careful about mortgages that have lower interest rates but include "points" that you have to pay up front. A "point" is just 1% of the purchase price in pre-paid interest. So, in this case, you're actually paying the interest up front, rather than over time, which usually isn't optimal. It means higher closing costs as well.

A final factor to consider when buying a home is whether to involve a realtor. These days, younger buyers like the freedom and flexibility of searching online and going to open houses at the start of their journey, rather than having to work around a realtor's schedule. I've had them show up at my open houses and say, "We really like the home. Now we just have to find a realtor and we'll be in touch." That makes little sense though—the realtor's job is to find you a home. You already found one! Many work under the false assumption that the realtor is free to buyers. I always remind them that if they bring in a realtor, I have to pay that commission, which will hurt their bargaining power accordingly. So, in reality, they are paying the realtor, not me. A realtor may also try to divert them to properties that the realtor has listed, meaning they'd earn both sides of the commission (buyer and seller sides). All these prospective buyers have to do is hire a great home inspector and real estate attorney. I go into much more detail on this in my aforementioned book *Show and Sell 2023*.

That said, realtors work hard for their money, and bring great expertise, a keen eye, and knowledge of the local market. Especially for first-time home buyers, a good realtor can be a tremendous asset. They typically earn a 3% commission when any homes they have listed sell (listing a home is the easy part of their job) and a 3% commission when they find a buyer for a home (as we'll discuss in the section on selling your home, this is negotiable in most cases!). Dealing with home buyers and schlepping them around to look at properties is the hard part of the job! If you're going to hire a realtor, use unbiased review sites like Google and Yelp to find a good one. The reviews on some realty-oriented sites can be biased. Don't use a realtor that does it part time, or just because they're a friend, neighbor, acquaintance, cousin, or whatever. Buying a home is a big deal. Don't compromise on any part of it. Don't let a realtor or anyone else talk you into even ***looking*** at homes outside your price range.

At the start of your home buying journey, spend a lot of time shopping online at zillow.com, realtor.com, redfin.com, and comparable sites. Learn the ropes of comparing properties by the key metrics, such as price per square foot. Set filters on those sites to be notified when the type of home you're looking for comes on the market. Go to some open houses and browse around. Ask questions. You'll learn a lot in a hurry, and dial in what you think you want in a home. There will probably be a realtor hosting the open house, and they'll certainly ask if you have a realtor yet, then give you the hard-sell. Stand firm. Do your research first before hiring someone for this important job!

Selling a Home

So, you want to sell the old "forever home," eh? Told you there was no such thing! Have you thought about doing an addition or renovations instead? Selling, then finding a new place, then moving is a big, expensive, stressful, complicated process. Make sure this isn't an emotional decision. Assess the alternatives. Consider the costs involved (on all those fronts) and make sure you're financially prepared. Don't upend your regular or financial life unless you're sure you're ready on the money side of things.

To Realtor or Not to Realtor?

We just discussed this from the buying perspective. It's a much bigger decision on the selling side, because you'll be the one forking over that big fat commission payment! It's a sizeable chunk of the valuable equity in your home. Realtors work hard, but most of that work is with prospective buyers. When you hire someone to help sell your home, they typically limit their work to pricing, coming up with (hopefully!) good listing text/photos, and maybe hosting one open house for you on a Sunday from 1pm-4pm. Most people can do it all themselves. When you factor in the huge commission savings, it's a handsome-paying part-time gig.

Realtors used to have a monopoly on selling homes, because you could only get your home in the MLS (Multiple-Listing Service) comprehensive book of homes for sale by signing up a realtor to sell your house. There was no internet, no Zillow or Trulia or Redfin or CraigsList. Without that MLS listing, you and your crappy red-and-white "For Sale by Owner" sign were virtually invisible to almost every person out there looking to buy a home.

Like so many others, this profession has been disrupted by technology, and that barrier is gone. Instead of paying 6% ransom to get that coveted MLS listing, you can buy one for a few hundred bucks. I bought my last one from simplechoicerealty.com. We all walk around with professional-level cameras in our pockets (however, don't discount the value of pro pics since most folks start their shopping online!). You know your home better than anyone, hence you can write a great summary and pitch about just why you bought it in the first place, and all the things you love about it. Have an open house every weekend, which would be a massive advantage over the other homes for sale that you are competing with. You can also hit up BuildASign.com and have a very nice yard sign made inexpensively. One that features your actual house, not the realtor kind that is just an ad for the realty company along with a big Photoshop-filtered 30-year-old picture of your smiling realtor. Get a hanging brochure box to place under that sign, and put it out by the edge of the property, cuz people are shy.

If a neighboring community has poorer schools or other disadvantages to yours, you are free to give those talking points to prospective buyers. A realtor might not, because they probably have listings for sale in those areas. Ok, I'm getting ahead of myself a bit. Let's work through the home-selling process in phases. When I listed my homes with flat-fee services, I indicated I would pay a realtor (that brought in a buyer) a 2% commission, and that's what I did. If you're going to use a realtor instead, I'd negotiate the commissions down to 2% listing and 2% buyer-side. 4% versus 6% is a big deal on a home sale.

Pricing Your Home

This part is super important. It's also where most people blow it, right out of the gate. If you price too high, it will be clear to any realtor, as well as the algorithms on websites that list homes for sale. They will flag it as over-valued. People might see that and remove it or never add it to their "likes" list and consideration. You truly don't get a second chance to make a first impression here! The price cannot simply be what you want to get for the house. The home/property is worth what it's worth, period. Some folks actually list low, in order to sell quickly, and perhaps even spark a bidding war that will drive the sale to an inflated price!

So, how do you find the magical number? First, check the Zillow zEstimate and realtor.com RealEstimate. Realtors will tell you those numbers are garbage, and they often are. Why? Because those websites rarely have accurate info about the home. When they do, though, their estimates are very accurate. Your first job is to go to those two websites and find the page for your property, then click the link that asks if you own the home. They will run you through some verification steps, and after you pass, you can then update the pages with complete and correct info. After that, give it a few days to marinate, and your estimates should be spot-on. You might start out 20% higher than that, in order to provide some negotiating wiggle-room. Check the price against comparable homes in your area (save these, they'll come in handy later). Does it look right? Be objective! Be wary of realtors that will try to lure you in by giving you an over-inflated number they say they can sell your house for. The price is the price is the price. Period.

List your home at the top-end of a range, not the bottom. For example, buyers will commonly search for homes less than $200,000. Setting your price at $200,000 leaves you out. Setting it at $199,500 puts you in. Also, don't go nuts with renovations. Most of them don't pay off (kitchens and bathrooms do, with exceptions). Pools can be a deterrent—not everyone wants the expense and hassle of caring for them, or the extra insurance costs.

Prepping Your Home

You're now living in a model home. Act like it! Start by decluttering everything—closets, countertops, basement, attic. It's a great time to put all that unused stuff up for sale on the online marketplaces we talked about in the Making More Moolah chapter. When we sold our last home, we ended up with an envelope stuffed with thousands of dollars in cold, hard cash, tax-free. It paid our closing costs!

You might also grab a temporary storage unit to put things out of the way until you're sold and moving out. You'll be ahead of the game there and thank yourself for it at moving time. It's essential to de-pet the place, as far as odors and maybe even the pets themselves, temporarily. If people see them, they will assume there is damage under the carpets. Litter boxes aren't a good look. You might not even notice the smells from your own pets, but others will. There are great deodorizers out there to fix the problem. Consider a professional cleaning service—they're usually inexpensive and well worth the money.

I said not to go crazy with home improvements, but fix things that need attention. You don't want buyers going away saying, "Loved it, but the driveway was a mess." Be judicious. Go through the home as a team, with a pencil and notepad, and make a list. While you're doing that, make notes about the outstanding features in each area of the house. Make sure the landscaping is up to snuff.

You might also remove your family pictures and mementos. Sorry! You want buyers to visualize the home as theirs, not yours. Definitely take down sports team, political, or religious items. I know New York Giants fans that would remove a home from consideration simply because of that Dallas Cowboys poster in the man-cave! As well, remove any valuables from drawers, jewelery boxes, and other hiding places, or make sure they're locked up.

If there are problems or concerns, for example, the HVAC is old, consider throwing a home warranty into the deal for buyers. You might also keep in mind that people become more active buyers toward the end of a school year, wanting to buy and get settled before the new term begins.

Marketing Your Home

It's important to have great pictures! Check your phone or camera settings to ensure the best quality. Make sure each area is very well lit. Wait for a sunny day and open those blinds to let the sunlight flood in. Buy 100-watt LED lights—they will come in handy to light the house during showings as well. Label each picture according to which room it is. It can be confusing for buyers trying to navigate the photos on your listing, so supply the context by naming the file, i.e. MasterBedroom.jpg and supplying a caption when you post them—"This is your spacious, sunlit master bedroom!"

If rooms are empty, or you've already moved out, there are virtual staging companies that will take your pictures and insert beautiful home furniture and decor for a modest price. These show better than pictures of an empty room. There are also companies that will bring in temporary staging furniture for your showings.

A big marketing tool is that front-yard sign I mentioned earlier. Have a nice one made. They come with metal brackets that you can drive into the lawn. Don't forget to make up one-page (front and back) color brochures. Free tools like Canva have great templates to use. If you don't have a good color printer, put the PDF on a thumb drive and bring it to Staples or another office store to get them printed out in bulk. Don't let that brochure box under your yard sign go empty!

When you're doing open houses, fly those colorful balloons, and try to post temp signs at strategic intersections near your home to direct folks your way. Get a combination lockbox so you can allow realtors to show your home when you aren't there. This allows them to enter the numeric combination, and pop open the lock to get to your house key inside.

You might also make business-cards with the key info and best photo, and stick those up on the bulletin boards at every grocery store, restaurant, and other places around your community. Hand them out to anyone you can chat up while you're out and about. Almost everyone knows someone who is thinking about buying a house soon. You might even offer a bounty, or finders-fee to any friends, coworkers, or others if they send a buyer your way. It beats paying a realtor commission!

Post your home as for-sale on Zillow, Realtor, Facebook, Nextdoor, craigslist, and anywhere else you can think of online. Go for maximum exposure! Have a year's worth of utility bills printed out for browsers to flip through to get an idea of heating/cooling costs.

These days, with the recent pandemic and all, it's fashionable to post a video walk-through of the home. Give a grand tour while you're doing it. You'll probably need a script and a few takes to get it just right. You might even consider getting a nice overhead drone video of the property and any nearby amenities (parks, pools, recreational sites like walking trails).

Showing Your Home

Whether it's during an open house, or showing driven by a buyer that's asked to come have a look-see, your home has to be ready. This can happen on short notice, so the key is to always be in show condition. That can be tough with a bunch of kids on the prowl! One thing you don't want to do is go crazy with scents of any kind—candles, plug-in room fresheners, etc. It can be annoying to people with sensitive sniffers, and people will assume you're trying to cover something up. A better idea is to have a good stash of ready-to-bake cookies in your fridge (the kind you slice and throw on a baking pan). That accomplishes two goals—the house smells homey and you have a delightful treat to give your potential buyers.

Go through each room prior to the buyers arriving. Make sure each light is on, flush the toilets, make everything sparkling clean. Send the kids and pets off somewhere for a while, if you can. Play some soft music, but not too loud.

Rehearse your home tour with family members. You may have already mastered it if you've done a home tour video. Give them the opportunity to ask questions. Don't be afraid to ask them how they like the home at the end! Even if it's a pass, you may mine lots of good intel.

Only show your home during daylight hours, and have someone else there with you. You can even vet your prospective buyers in advance by asking for mortgage pre-approval or pre-qualification and identifying information. Make sure you let someone know who is coming over and when.

You might also offer to step aside and let the buyers go through one more time on their own. This is a matter of trust, of course. Is everything of value locked up? Do you get a good vibe from them? Do you have security cameras running? If you're not comfortable with things like this, a realtor may be a better choice than selling on your own.

Open Houses

Realtors will usually do open houses from 1-4pm on Sundays. That means you're competing with every single other open house at the same time. If you're selling on your own, you can be strategic! I had mine from noon to 5pm or later and caught plenty of overflow from those other open houses. I had some on Saturdays, and a few on weeknights after work hours.

Make sure you have hand soap, hand towels, a can of air freshener, and a plunger in each bathroom. Put out some bottled water and snacks. Be careful about anything that can stain or do damage, because people will bring their kids! Make it a fun, festive atmosphere if you can. Think about the parking in advance. Keep an eye out the front door and windows for those lookie-lous that might be nervous about coming in. Step out and offer an invitation!

Many early lookers may not have a realtor yet. You might ask them and remind them if they don't they can get a better deal on the property by simply hiring a real estate attorney and good home inspector.

After each tour, go back through the house and turn on the lights they will have turned off, clean up and restore order. Recheck those toilets!

Show and Sell 2023 has a lot more detail, plus pictures, and has plenty of humorous stories of things that happened during my open houses and home showings. People!

Closing the Deal

Hey, you got an offer! Now what!? Keep in mind, with any offer, buyers will come in low and expect negotiation. Circumstances can vary depending on whether you're in a buyer or seller market. *Show and Sell 2023* goes into both scenarios in detail. Have some things in mind that you can concede to sweeten the deal without giving up too much price-wise (like a home warranty, they're pretty inexpensive).

Vet any offer—is the buyer pre-qualified or pre-approved (the better one)? Do they have credit reports? Have they been in their jobs for more than a year? How much cash will they be putting down as a deposit (typically 1% earnest money to start, but also how much when they close?). If they're going to pay cash, don't be shy about asking for proof they have the money sitting in an account, and aren't depending on an on-the-sly loan from good old Uncle Charlie.

You should have a good realty attorney. If you don't, now's the time to find one. Ask them to review any offer or contract. If the buyer has a realtor, you have to pay that commission (negotiated to 2%, remember?) but the bonus is that they'll guide the process. Remember, they work for the buyers, but it's in their best interest to not make waves and get the deal done, so they can get to their payday. If your buyer doesn't have a realtor, the company you did your flat-fee listing through usually has a transaction concierge type service that involves them shepherding you through the deal from start to finish. If not, hire a company to do that if you need it. Your realty attorney typically will handle most, if not all, the steps.

Negotiate. Be creative. Everything is negotiable. Think about leaving appliances behind if the buyers don't have them. Then you can buy new ones! Be very careful about contingencies, such as the buyers have to find a buyer for their home first. If theirs is overpriced, that could take a while. Maybe wait for a buyer that doesn't have that problem, such as first-time home buyers. Don't get roped into paying the buyer's closing costs, unless it's a very extreme buyer's market and you have little choice.

Update your home listings as "offer-pending," then "under contract," and "sold" each step of the way. Keep showing it and taking offers, in case the deal falls through!

CHAPTER EIGHT

Buying and Selling Vehicles

DON'T GET RIPPED OFF

"The road to riches is this simple: Drive a crappy car."

Jared Dillian

We're saying 'vehicles' in the chapter title because the same advice applies whether you're buying/selling a car, RV, boat, plane, or any other. Let's start with the buying side first.

Buying New Vehicles

Listen, we all love that new car smell. It's nice getting a shiny ride right off the assembly line and showroom floor, all up to date with the latest gadgets and tech. Be patient. If you do the right thing now, the rest of your life can be full of a never-ending series of new cars, paid for with cash. Doing it before you can afford it by taking a loan, or worse yet a lease, will only keep you on that work hamster wheel longer. You'll pay a lot more for insurance. And, yeah granny or junior will run a shopping cart (or seven) into it within weeks. You can't hide from them. Parking on the outskirts of the lot only makes them angrier. Granny might bust out her keys.

When I was young and just getting started in life fresh from military and working my way through college, I drove very-used cars. I was always paranoid about them breaking down, because I had little kids, so I saved up a repair fund. Soon, that repair fund grew to be enough to buy my next car. Since that period, my lifelong approach to this is to buy well-loved, almost brand new cars. I let someone else take that immediate depreciation hit. I pay cash (huge bargaining point!) and drive them for five or more years, taking excellent care of them, and often sell them for close to what I paid for them. Who says cars are expensive? I use consumerreports.org's wonderful guide to the best used cars in each price bracket—it has never failed me.

I've bought motorcycles, a boat, and a recreational vehicle by using the techniques in this chapter, and sold all of them for more than I paid, after enjoying them for years. It's hard to understand people walking into dealerships and getting talked into financing agreements and huge payments, or worse, leasing. Especially when they have dreams in life.

Case Study: I had a single young lady client who was doing so well. She had wiped out most of her debt in a gazelle-intense fashion. She was on her way to a different life, and out of the old stressed-out one. Then she called to tell me she had bought a new car and was in love with it. She went in for that infamous inexpensive oil change at the dealer. They took her for a test ride while she waited and offered a "deal she couldn't resist." We did the math, and it meant not just the five years on the loan before she could reach her dream of being debt free—it had a snowball effect (the wrong way!) that meant it would take her seven years. She was within a year of paying off her debt, and then without the payments, she could have saved up enough pretty fast to buy that car with cash, and saved thousands of dollars.

You've likely heard that a new ride depreciates big-time the moment you drive it off the lot. Why not buy something a year or two old and let someone else take that hit? There are plenty of folks who trade up every other year to a new car. Do things right and you'll be one of them, right?

Oh, don't give me that "I need something safe and reliable!" line. Cars today are almost **all** safe and reliable until you get way down into the very bottom spectrum. And that's why you have that talented mechanic we talked about in Chapter 4. Stay on top of the maintenance, pay for AAA, and you'll be fine.

When the day comes and you're ready to new-car shop, use a service like Consumer Reports or TrueCar to find out exactly what the dealer pays (minus incentives and such) and start negotiating 5% up from there. Read the agreement carefully, and don't get sucked into the up-charge for silly things like undercoating. Places like Costco have services to get you pretty close to the best deal if you don't want to go through the negotiations. Be wary of trading in your old ride. Often dealers will offer a sweet trade-in price to lure you in, but turn around and tack extra money on the cost of the car you're buying to replace it.

Leasing. Don't do it, unless you have some unusual sweet deal from your employer or other. It's the most expensive way to own a car according to Car & Driver and Consumer Reports. Studies have shown it's roughly equivalent to a 14% loan. You wouldn't get a car loan at 14%, would you? (Would you??). Sure, the payments look lower than loan payments, but after a loan you get to keep the car. And, you don't get dinged for mileage charges and all the other ways they have to put a hurt on you with a lease. Wait until we talk about investing and you see how much wealth you can build by investing those payments instead.

Buying Used Vehicles

Let's break down the process to find a great used vehicle. Step-by-step!

Step 1: Teamwork! Refer to Chapter 4, when we talked about the value of having a relationship with a good, honest, independent local mechanic. As in, one that doesn't work for a new or used car dealer. This is where that relationship pays off in spades. First, ask them to keep an eye out for you, in case any vehicles they're familiar with come on the market. They often have customers give them an early heads-up. Second, ask them to evaluate your current ride, if you're going to sell it. Ask them to help you find a buyer!

Step 2: Get Organized. Set a realistic budget for yourself. In the best case, you've been preparing and saving for this with a dedicated savings/sinking fund. Don't overshoot it by falling in love with something out of your price range. This is a big purchase. Don't sacrifice those days (years?) of financial freedom! What kind of car are you looking for? Truck? SUV? 2-door coupe? 4-door sedan? Once you have an idea, get a copy of the April issue of Consumer Reports at your local library or online. That's the annual car issue. They usually list the best and worst used cars, by type, in each price range. Bingo! There's your candidate list, all narrowed down! Create a one-page form called Vehicle Prospects and print off a bunch of copies. It should contain places to put:

Vehicle Make/Model/Year:

Price:

VIN:

nada.com/kbb.com private party value:

Phone #:

Why selling:

Mileage:

Options (auto/standard, power/air/cd/etc):

How long been for sale:

How many owners:

Ever wrecked/flooded:

Any major repairs done:

Two sets of keys?

Any major repairs needed:

Date of inspection:

Clean non-salvage title or lien/loan?

Address where the vehicle is located:

carfax.com or autocheck.com report available? (get your own!)

Also, have a few copies of a deposit form and bill of sale form. You can find free ones online, and we provide them with our class on this topic.

Step 3: Search. Now head to the usual spots. Private party sales are your best deal. That means going to Facebook Marketplace, nextdoor.com, OfferUp, craigslist.org, autotrader.com, cycletrader.com, rvtrader.com, etc. Set search filters on those sites with the vehicles in your list, so you're notified immediately if any become available. Tag any that are currently available, make calls, fill out your prospect sheets. Other non-private party options are carvana.com, vroom.com, and carmax.com. You won't get as good a deal as private-party, but usually better than standard dealers or used-car lots.

Do as much of this over the phone as you can. You want to narrow the list down to only prime contenders before you take the time-consuming trips to go look at the cars in person. It's not worth wasting that time if you've discovered the vehicle has a salvage title over the phone.

Step 4: Visit/Drive. Most importantly, be safe. Rather than go to someone's home to check out a vehicle, consider having them meet you in a shopping center or municipal parking lot (daytime only, of course) where there are likely surveillance cameras and maybe room to drive around the lot. If you can, bring someone with you to act as a scribe. Jot down notes and take pictures. You want to first visually check the vehicle from front to back, top to bottom, carefully. Look for any minor problems, like chips in the windshield, slight dents, scratches, etc. Note how much tread is left on the tires—all of them! Push down hard on the front and back. If it bobs more than once, it may need a new suspension. Push hard side-to-side on each corner and the wheels. Any unusual noises? If it has locking wheel lugs, is the key there? Any oily residue in the exhaust tailpipe?

Check the trunk—any mold or mildew signs or smells? Pull up any lining to look for signs of rust or repainting. Is the spare tire there, if that model came with one? The tire change kit or any other accessories? Pop the hood. Check the wiper fluid levels, check the oil dipstick for any grittiness in the oil. The antifreeze/coolant should be green or orange. Any corrosion on the battery and terminals? Are the belts cracked and worn?

Now make sure everything is functional. You should not get in the car with anyone you don't know. Ask the owner to get in, then stand outside and ask them to operate the wipers, lights, directional signals while you stand in front of or behind the car. Next you should get in, alone, and check the heat/air and other interior features. It's a trick by sellers to sell a car that needs expensive heat repairs during summer, when buyers are unlikely to check that. And vice versa for selling vehicles with broken air conditioners in winter! Have a look at the gas/brake pedals. If they're worn, but the odometer says something low, like 30,000, they may have rolled the mileage back. Ask to see two sets of keys—replacements are crazy expensive these days.

If nothing has ruled the vehicle out yet, it's time for a test drive. Never go with the owner! Run the car through its paces. Accelerate and listen for noises. It should be smooth. Brake hard. It should brake straight. Keep the radio off so you can hear subtle sounds. Take hard turns in both directions. Drive safely! Head straight at slow speed and take your hands off the wheel (empty parking lot recommended). Does the car stay straight, or is there perhaps an alignment problem? Try as many features as you can. Take your time.

If you think you have a winner, ask what the bottom line is. Don't appear anxious. Most sellers list their cars around 20% higher than their bottom line. Negotiate. Play hardball. Don't be afraid to state your best offer, and even if they decline, make sure they have your number or email and ask them to reach out if they reconsider.

If it's truly "the one," get that deposit form handy. It should state that you're leaving a good-faith deposit (usually $100 or so) for being able to have your trusted mechanic check the car over before you complete the deal. You could even have a local from yourmechanic.com come to the seller's location and check the car, but it won't be as thorough as your own mechanic in their shop. If the seller has a loan on the car, you're going to have to trust them to take your money, pay off the loan, and then get the title to you.

When you take possession of the vehicle, make sure everything is still in place, including both sets of keys, the manual, and anything else that goes with it.

Selling Your Vehicle

First, avoid trading in. You'll get less because the dealer has to give you a wholesale price in order to sell it at a profit for what it's really worth. If they give you an inflated price, they're probably making that up on the sale of a replacement car to you. If you still have a loan on your car, make sure you have enough cash to pay it off, along with your bottom line price. The buyer will want that title ASAP!

Step 1: Prepare. Have your trusted mechanic go over the car to detect any problems. Fix them. Get the fluids changed. Let your mechanic know you'll pay them a finder's fee if they get you a buyer. Give any prospective buyers your mechanic's number. Have the car detailed, it's an expense that pays for itself to have it showroom-clean. It should cost $150-200 for that. If the tires are anywhere near worn out, replace them with an inexpensive (but good quality) set. Remove any personal stuff, bumper stickers, or clutter. Clean out the trunk, glove box, and other storage areas. Next, take some great pictures on a nice, sunny day.

Get your docs in order—manual, repair records, title/registration, insurance card, Carfax/Autocheck report, printouts of the NADA/KBB values for the vehicle. Find reviews for that specific year/make/model and crib the positive comments for your ads and sales spiel, especially the Consumer Reports review/rating from the year the vehicle came out. Set your price about 20% above what the fair market private party value is from KBB/NADA. Just for giggles, you might see what carvana.com and vroom.com will give you. It's an online process that takes just a few minutes, and they'll come pick it up.

Step 2: Post. Get it posted on some (or all!) of the online marketplaces that we mentioned in the section on buying a vehicle. Use enticing terms like "well-loved," "garage-kept," "meticulously maintained," and anything else that may touch people's emotions.

Step 3: Meet and Greet. When prospects call, give all the info you can and be honest, so only solid ones show up to take your time in-person. Daytime showings only, and again, perhaps away from your home in a public place such as a police dept parking lot. Crooks don't like it there! Give a walking tour around the outside of the car, pointing out the highlights and things you love about it. Be suspicious of anyone that doesn't show up in a vehicle, because it's your collateral when they take yours on a test drive! You might request to see their license and insurance card and take a picture of those and the buyer before they take your car for a test drive. Take a photo of their license plate. Make sure nothing valuable is in the car when they take it for a test drive, and check that everything is still in place when they return. Give them only the one car key, not your whole key ring with your house keys on it!

Step 4: Sell. Make sure to get a solid non-refundable cash deposit if someone is interested. Get a signed deposit form with the details. Set parameters to close the deal, no stalling. If they want their mechanic to check it out, you bring it there, rather than give them the car to joyride in for a day. Before you turn the vehicle over, make sure you have all your stuff out! ***Congratulations!***

CHAPTER NINE

(Not) Paying for Higher Ed

FIND A WAY NOT TO PAY!

"Education is the way out of the poverty trap. It shouldn't be the poverty trap itself and make those trying to better themselves incur massive student debt."

Stewart Stafford

No, no, not the 'higher Ed' kid who used to sleep in the back of history class in high school. Higher Education! Oh, boy, this can be an enormous expense. We just talked about homes being one of the biggest expenses in your financial life, but sending one or multiple kids off to learn beer pong can top the home purchase. Again, we live in one of the few major countries where higher education isn't at least somewhat or totally free. Let's fight back. Make it free! The advice in this chapter isn't just for college. It also applies to trade and technical schools, and I discuss those as viable options. The steps you can take start as early as 7th grade, as you'll see!

What Not to Do

Let's start off on the right foot, here. Both parents and prospective students make plenty of mistakes in the very early stages. Please don't push (passively or aggressively) your kids to go to a school just because you did, because you like the sports teams, or it's the "family tradition." Don't bias yourself because you want bragging rights to your friends. "Status" is an enormous factor in financial failure, whether it's a big home or shiny car you can't afford or ivy-covered buildings at your kids' school. Don't sacrifice your wonderful golden years and retirement!

Don't let your kids pick a school because *they* like the sports teams, or "it's in a pretty town," or "it's close to the beach" (Son, you'll be home, working all summer!). A lot of high-school kids want to go somewhere their friends are going. Remind them that many of these schools are the size of small cities, and they may never see those old high school chums. They will probably make new ones, and travel in different social circles.

Fun story—I went into the military after high school with my best friend under the "buddy program" and never saw the guy again after boot camp, and that wasn't exactly a social environment. I'm sure the recruiter had a good laugh. Anyway, I digress. Also, don't let your kids pick a school because of its high ranking on the annual "best party schools" list. That's not what "the experience" should be about.

Help them write a list of criteria for what they want to study and what they're looking for in a school. Whatever you do, don't attach assets like your home to college debt by financing it with a HELOC. Don't take money out of your retirement plan. We'll discuss plenty of ways to avoid that in this chapter.

Have an honest conversation with your kids. These days, many are disavowing the whole "rounded education" thing, seeing many schools for the corporate profit factories they are, and getting targeted learning either online (Udemy, Coursera, etc) or at specialty schools, then entering the workforce early while their friends are racking up student loan debt and vomiting out of windows.

Case Study: I had a client who said they made fun of him in high school because he transferred to the vo-tech (vocational-technical) school. They called him dumb, and worse. He learned the electrical trade there, and got hired as a union member right out of high school. He quickly saved up enough money to start out on his own. By the time he was in his 40s, he was enjoying driving up to his high school reunions in his brand-new Porsche (he upgraded every other year) and listening to the sob stories from the "smart" kids about how they were still trying to pay off their student loans. He now owns a local chain of electrical service providers. Moral of the story: don't spend all that money on college if your kids aren't into it.

Don't push your kids to higher education if they're not ready or are resisting. You'll waste tons of money. They won't "adapt." If they want a gap year, fine. Let them know it won't be spent running around full time to Burning Man and other festivals "finding themselves." They'll be working, paying rent, and yes, they should be paying for their own car insurance, cell phones, and other costs after high school. Allow them to be actual adults! Entering the military can be a great thing, as can joining organizations like the Peace Corps. They may just find themselves, as these can be character-shaping experiences.

Case Study: I had a client whose daughter wasn't sure she was ready or knew what she wanted to study after high school. They were also short on funding, so the daughter went to work for a gas station/convenience store chain that gives money for college as a benefit. After a year, she was already working her way into the management ranks and knew what she wanted to do. She's going to community college for business part-time while continuing as a manager at the store. She's living at home and saving money instead of piling up student loan debt.

Case Study: My eldest daughter went to community college after high school, and quickly determined it wasn't for her (even though she was a good student). She went into the workforce and worked her way up the ladder to a position managing large teams. She's done very well for herself.

Student Debt

Be aware that when they turn 18, your kids can apply for all the credit cards, student loans, and other credit they want. They don't need your signature. There will be plenty of predatory lenders around their school campus waiting to pounce. Make sure you're clear on this with them. You might even demand a peek at their free credit report a few times a year. Talk to them about this before the time comes, and draw up an informal, signed agreement. It's an intro to adult life! Make sure their education starts with an education (from you) about the perils of debt. Maybe give them a copy of this book for pre-higher ed summer reading :-)

Student loans should be a last resort. We'll show you many ways to avoid them at all costs. But if they're used, be strategic and make sure they're only for essential costs—tuition and books, not spring break in Cancun. If you're doing parent loans, make sure any agreement is in writing with your kids. I've seen plenty of cases where it was "agreed" that the kids would pick up the payments after they joined the workforce, but when the time came, had no recollection of such a deal. This can cause family fractures.

If the plan is to go to work in an altruistic environment to take advantage of Public Service Loan Forgiveness, such as serving in needy communities after graduation, make sure you know the rules in advance. Have a backup plan in case it doesn't happen, for whatever reason. Keep in mind that student loans aren't bankruptible, except in very rare circumstances! They're the "gift" that keeps on giving.

So, have that talk with your kids. Remind them that a $100,000 loan at 6% with a ten-year repayment schedule will mean they'll start their career with a $1,100 monthly loan payment. So much for that nice car or apartment they wanted to reward themselves with! If they get a $50,000 starter salary, that will be 26% of their income before taxes. They'll pay $133,200 total, and that's a new-car's worth of interest. Sober them with those numbers! They'll be "ancient," in their mid-thirties if they're lucky, before it's paid off.

One rule of thumb is to never borrow more (total) than they expect to make in their first year's salary in the job they're studying for. My rule of thumb is to avoid debt, in case I haven't made that clear!

Typical Costs

Way back in 1989, you could get a 4-year degree at a state/public university for $26,000 total. Today, it's over $100,000—four times more! Private college tuition went from $28,440 a year to more than $40,000 a year on average. More if you want ivy-covered buildings, of course. Tuition costs have been outpacing wage increases by eight times. Since the pandemic, that's abated some, as schools have been forced to adopt virtual options, which of course cost them far less, and thus allows for price cuts. The number of students choosing other options (as discussed above) has also forced them to rethink these drastic hikes.

Average annual tuition costs in 2018 were about $4,000/year for in-state community college/trade/tech schools, $20,000 for in-state public universities, $30,000 for out-of-state public universities, and $40,000 for private schools. That's quite a disparity for often learning the same stuff! Note those numbers are *tuition*—tack on another $10k or more for room and board and other expenses, if they're not commuting. Do a recent, current cost analysis for any schools you're considering at sites like bigfuture.collegeboard.org/pay-for-college/calculate-your-cost/net-price-calculator, savingforcollege.com, or collegetuitioncompare.com.

Community College

Did you know that 79% of millionaires didn't attend a prestigious college?

The first two years of college is typically general education and prerequisites. Why spend top dollar on those basic subjects? Especially if your 18-year-old isn't ready (either by your assessment or theirs) to be away from the comforts of home yet. They probably don't know what they want to major in yet anyway, and even if they do, it usually changes by the junior year of college. Save the money and have them start out local, at one of our amazing two-year community colleges. It's a good way to go even if they just want a two-year degree. Most schools have both college prep and job training tracks.

That's how I started, at good old Tulsa Jr. College in Oklahoma. I'll never forget those years. I could stretch my GI Bill benefits and have enough left to do my final years at a great 4-year school. Let your kids know that this might be the recipe that works if they want to graduate with their 4-year degree from a more expensive school than they (or you) can afford. It may be safer, and help to prevent them from being exposed to the downside of college life (stress, loneliness, partying, pranks, shenanigans, being overwhelmed) before they're ready.

In fact, when two of my kids graduated high school, they weren't ready for the big-house up in Happy Valley, PA (Penn State) so they started out at satellite campuses for Penn State that were essentially two-year community colleges that the university bought out and put their name on. It was a much more manageable situation for them, and less expensive to start out that way. More details later. Go this way, and you may have a better shot at the aid and scholarships we'll discuss later.

If you go this route intending to transfer to a 4-year school for the junior/senior years, make sure the two schools work together and all credits will be transferrable.

Sources of Funding

There are many ways to help pay for higher education. Much more so for the kids than the parents! You want me to prove it? OK, here we go.

Sources of Funding for Students

- Loans

- Grants

- Scholarships

- Research assistantships

- Teaching assistantships

- Work study

- Formal co-op program

- Internships

- ROTC (summer training pay, free college, even if you quit the program in the first year!)

- Resident advisor (free housing + meals + living stipend)

- On-campus jobs during school year

- Summer jobs between college semesters

- Jobs during the school year in high school or during HS summer breaks

- Entrepreneurship

- UTMA investment accounts

They have nights, weekends, breaks, and a three-month summer vacation to figure out ways to make money!

Sources of Funding for Parents (Ready?)
- 529 College Savings Plans

- Retirement portfolio (No!)

- Part-time job, freelancing, blogging, consulting, entrepreneurship (Ugh!)

- Investment accounts

The moral of that story is to make sure they have some skin in the game, even if you're wealthy. They may be more conscientious about going to class and making good grades. It's character building. They'll have a great sob story to tell their kids, about how mean their parents were back in the day.

How to Pay Cash

There are two fundamental ways to pay cash—save up/invest and find free money. Always check with your employer about any programs or benefits to help your kids with their education. Check with your kids' employer (they're working part-time in high school, right?). Sometimes, if you're a valued employee, they will make the money appear as an impromptu scholarship or bonus for you. It never hurts to ask. It might make them concerned you're going to find a higher paying job, or one with such benefits.

Another way to get "free" college classes is to make sure your child enrolls in any available dual-enrollment courses in high school. These are classes that will actually give them college credits! Each one you take correlates to credits you don't have to pay for later, and an earlier graduation from college, meaning savings on room/board, fees, and other costs. They might take summer semester classes right after high school graduation—those are shorter and often easier than regular semester classes.

There's also a program called the Modern States Education Alliance "Freshman Year for Free" at modernstates.org, which will allow for a free, virtual first year of college with credits transferrable to most any school after that. When you're vetting schools, ask the bursar/student aid office about any opportunities to join work-study programs, local apprenticeships or on-campus work (for the kids, not parents).

You might have noticed military ROTC (Reserve Officer Training Program) in the list above. Those programs offer pay for training, learning discipline, a possible later career path, and best of all, free college for those who sign up. Even if your child decides it's not for them and bails out early, they will often still pay for the first year of school. It's worth checking into!

Statistics show that students who work during high school and college get better grades and get in less trouble. It's not child abuse! It's teaching responsibility, accountability, and best of all, financial wellness. Higher education courses can be scheduled to allow for this. They might schedule more classes on Monday, Wednesday, and Friday and have Tuesday and Thursday off to work. Colleges like seeing a work history on the applications of high school students. As someone who did countless hiring interviews with kids just out of college, I can tell you the ones who had a record of working through college got more attention. It says a lot about them.

If you need help to motivate your kids to help with all the above, just tell them that if they bankrupt you or ruin your retirement with these education expenses, you'll have to stay with them when they're young, newly married, and in their first home. It's no fun having two sets of diapers to change!

Scholarships/Grants/Aid

Scholarships, grants, and aid are all free money—they don't have to be repaid. Grants and aid are typically needs-based, whereas scholarships are both need and merit-based, meaning wealthy families can also apply. These programs are first-come, first-served, and when the money is spoken for, there's no more until next year. That's why it's so important to get the jump early.

FAFSA (Free Application for Federal Student Aid) applications open up on October 1 each year, and that's exactly when you should apply! Common logic says to apply even if you think you're over the income limit for any aid—you might be surprised, and it's free to apply. You'll receive a letter in response that shows any help you'll get toward expenses, and what your "Expected Family Contribution" (EFC) is (how much you'll pay). It's a hack to always appeal that number! Sometimes you'll do even better. They changed the FAFSA in 2023 and it's now shorter and easier to fill out. Don't assume you make too much money. Fill it out!

Applying for scholarships can be a repetitive, mind-numbing, no-fun process. That's why it's good for your kids to do—it gets them ready for the real world! But, if done correctly, it'll be the best paying part-time job they ever have (and the same for you, while you're helping them—teamwork). This process is best done in an organized fashion, starting as soon as the junior year of high school. Set up a war room on the dining room table, and everyone gets a job. Look for ways to automate the process and re-use your inputs.

Starting in junior year of high school, spend an hour a day on this project, if possible. Remember, you're getting paid for the time. It teaches how to deal with rejection, and how to be patient. If your child won't do this work, how will they succeed with the workload of college, tech, or trade school? Are they truly ready? It's not unusual to get dozens of rejections before receiving that first, wonderful acceptance letter (which may pay for an entire semester of tuition).

There are countless websites to help you manage the scholarship application process and keep track of the ones you've submitted to. Some of them are horrible, some are fronts for other nefarious purposes, so be careful. A few to try are myscholly.com and pay ingforcollegeresource.com. Collegescholarships.org has reviews of many college search engines, check out the latest.

Most scholarships are free to apply to—question any that want money. Check your grammar carefully with tools like grammarly .com and prowritingaid.com. Read your essay responses out loud to yourself or others. There are three types of scholarships—academic, athletic, and character-based/specialty. Start local, because there's less competition. Check with local businesses, the Chamber of Commerce, your employers, utility companies, banks/credit unions, Elks/Rotary/Kiwanis/American Legion/Veteran's organizations. Pester your guidance counselors at high school for the best ones. Then move on to the national scholarships. There's more competition for those, but the awards are higher. Of course, check with any school that accepts you as a student. Here are a few more resources:

nerdwallet.com/blog/loans/student-loans/grants-for-college

nasfaa.org/State_Financial_Aid_Programs

nerdwallet.com/blog/loans/student-loans/how-to-get-a-scholarship

fastweb.com

careeronestop.org/toolkit/training/find-scholarships.aspx

529 and Coverdell ESA

There's not a lot to talk about here, as 529 college savings plans have far overtaken usage of the older Coverdell ESA plans. The ESA had disadvantages in terms of income restrictions, annual contribution amounts, and beneficiary age limits. So we'll skip those and talk about 529s.

Before you plow money into a 529, please make sure you're debt-free except your mortgage and have 3-6 months of expenses in an emergency fund. Those two things far outweigh college savings in the priority list. Help yourself first, so you can be in a better position to help them later (just like you put your own oxygen mask on first in the airplane). You can open a 529 in any state, it doesn't have to be the one you live in. Some state plans are better than others, but if you use one from your own state, you may get a state tax break. For example, NJ doesn't offer that tax break, so the residents there frequently open Pennsylvania 529 plans, which feature low-cost Vanguard funds. 529 plans aren't like your traditional 401k/403b/527 retirement plans—the amount you contribute isn't subtracted from your federal earned income. But the growth is tax-free as long as you use it for the intended and approved purposes.

If you can contribute just $2,000 per year from birth on, at an average 10% rate of return, you'd have over $100,000 at age 18. If your child doesn't go to higher education, you can then designate a sibling or other family member, including grandchildren, nieces, nephews, cousins, etc. Even yourself! Thanks to new legislation, you can roll it into a Roth IRA account after fifteen years. Otherwise, you'd have to pay a 10% penalty to take the money out, and they would tax the growth at income tax rates, not long-term capital gains rates.

The SECURE Act 2.0 now allows unused 529 money to be rolled into a Roth IRA, but there are strings. The 529 must have been open for at least 15 years (so, open one as early as possible even if not funding!), contributions within the prior five years to the rollover aren't eligible, has to go into a Roth in the name of the 529 beneficiary (not the 529 owner!), lifetime cap of $35k, must have earned income, and it counts against any eligible Roth contribution for the year.

529 Contrarian View

As we saw, the 529 has fewer strings than the Coverdell ESA. But, there are strings. Why not put the money in the same investments, but in a dedicated brokerage account? There are advantages to that strategy. For example, the fees are lower. Gains and qualified dividends are taxed, but at the preferable long-term capital gains rates if you hold shares longer than a year. The aid algorithms weigh the brokerage account and 529s equally when filing the FAFSA. For that reason, grandparents and other family members are often urged to not put money into 529 plans, rather just pay the schools directly when the time comes, if they want to help. The same recent legislation has changed that. Non-parent/guardian family member 529s don't count toward the EFC.

As I said earlier, you could take the money from your retirement accounts, as a qualified early withdrawal and hence no penalty. We said not to do that, so you don't end up living in your kid's basement when you're old. Two things that FAFSA algorithm doesn't look at are your retirement account and your home, in terms of your ability to pay. Knowing that, some folks have passed on the other approaches we discussed and just plowed money into paying the mortgage off early, loading up a separate dedicated IRA designated just for school money (and not counted toward any retirement plan calculations). Then, when junior heads off to school, they take a 4-year sabbatical from work (or, mini-retirement, or, actual early retirement). What does the FAFSA algorithm see? It sees people who have no income, limited assets (remember the house and retirement accounts are invisible). What does it determine? These folks need lots of aid/grants.

As an example, a family with $500k of 'visible' assets, half in a 529 and half in a brokerage account would have an expected family contribution (as of 2023 now called Student Aid Index, or SAI) of about $25,000/year. The same family with no (or low) income, no 529/brokerage, but a paid off home and $500k in retirement accounts would have an EFC of $0. You can adjust as necessary—do an internet search of EFC/SAI at different levels of adjusted gross income (AGI).

Standardized Tests

Standardized tests like the SAT and ACT are important for both admissions and aid/scholarship decisions. There used to be big differences between the two, but over time, they have revamped the SAT to look more like the ACT. Make sure you deploy a good test-taking strategy! Take a first pass by not spending too much time on questions you don't know the answer to, or may take more time. Then, as time allows, go back and focus on those with a second pass through the test. If you get to where there are still unanswered questions and you have no clue about them, statistically you'd do better by answering them all with the same letter, i.e. choice 'c'.

Take them early and often, starting with the 'practice' versions in freshman year of high school. The scores don't count until junior year/11th grade. It's good practice and helps deal with the stress factor. There are excellent test prep classes, both online and in person, and they're quite affordable. Because of newer super-scoring rules, only the best scores in each section will count. For example, if you do better on the math section in junior year, but better in the English section in senior year, you score out with those two combined. Monitor when they're available, as the schedules fill up quickly.

Some schools will prefer SAT, some prefer ACT. Know which ones your target schools like. There are tons of great practice materials available, and also some terrible ones. Hey, some kids aren't wired well for test-taking. It's not the end of the world. Colleges know that, and depending on their major, it might not be a big deal. Schools use other criteria for admission. Always communicate with the good people in the admissions office. Make a friend there by being courteous, friendly, and not overly pesky.

Timing: 6th Grade Through Diploma

There are many ideas below, as far as how to prepare your kids for higher education and how to get the most free money. No matter what, make sure they know they're loved at every stage of life. We often forget how stressful and overwhelming these years can be for pre-teens and teens. They have a lot going on socially and emotionally. If you go overboard with any of this and cause them excessive stress, the results can be the opposite of what you're trying to achieve.

6th-7th Grade. What things can you do to improve your odds of admission and getting all that free money? They're moving out of childhood. It's time to dream/visualize their future. What job do they think they'd love to go to every day? Have those conversations, but as a parent, pay attention to their hobbies and interests. Take those guidance department aptitude test and discuss the results. An important box to check in these early years is membership in the Junior National Honor Society (6th through 9th grade).

8th Grade. Continue matching hobbies/interests to potential careers. Now they can start picking their classes in school—make good choices! As a parent, start learning about scholarships and their requirements. Keep reminding them about character—all the hard work and dreams can disappear with one awful friend or decision. Pay close attention to their circle of friends. Are they good influences? Take the PSAT when it becomes available.

9th Grade. It's officially high school time! Grades matter big-time now. Take those harder advanced placement courses. Focus on honors/college prep classes, as the subject matter is more in-depth. Do these throughout high school. Kids begin to feel more adult, as they should, because of their lofty high school stature. Until the upper classes take them down a notch or ten, of course. It can be a rough change. The work gets harder.

Get them any help they need, communicate every day, get them to open up. Remind them that social media is now open game as far as the higher education schools are concerned. An unfortunate post might cost them admission to the school of their dreams. If they don't already have a professional email address such as first.lastname@gmail.com, create one. You don't want iloveboob s@yahoo.com on their scholarship applications.

Reach out and build relationships with the guidance department and teachers, make sure your child understands how important those references will be later! Having a part-time job, maybe some entrepreneurial activity (even if it's a failed one, or simple lawn mowing/pet care), and activities/volunteerism are important, but don't overdo it. Things like model United Nations, debate team, mentoring, science bowls, foreign language club/trips, arts, community service stand out on applications. Document all these hours and activities.

You might even find scholarships you can apply for at this stage. Start looking! Do **not** get them a credit card to teach "financial responsibility." It's like "Here, I'm going to give you a bomb-making kit to show you how people can get blown up by fooling around with bombs." Teach them the value of saving for things they want, making money, and the discount and simplicity of paying in cash (even if it's with a debit card). They should have their own bank account. Add them as an authorized user on your card for emergencies and oversight. That also helps build their credit profile.

10th Grade. Advanced Placement courses should be available by now at most high schools. Take them! Apply to more scholarships. Check into the National Honor Society and start heading to college admissions fairs—they can be a good bang for the buck in terms of value for your time spent. Start a list of school choices and pros/cons. Enjoy this year, it's the calm before the storm!

11th Grade. Ah, the main event. SAT/ACT test scores officially count now! Dual enrollment courses should be available. They're a real money-saver and look great on the transcript! Whittle down the list of schools and be honest about which may not be viable. Start those visits, including public/in-state colleges, community colleges, tech schools, and trade schools. Go when classes are in session to get a feel for the campus vibe. Lots of drunk kids hanging upside down from balconies? Eat in the cafeteria. Meet with professors/teachers and admissions staff. Check out the dorms and rules. Get the low-down on the full, actual cost of attendance, including all fees, and ask about aid/scholarships. Start sending in early admission applications to the most desired schools.

12th Grade. Ah, senioritis! How many kids blew it after all those years of work just by doing something malicious to the rival school, or a night out after getting an older friend to buy alcohol? Keep on them about consequences. Don't let them buy into the myth that after they're accepted by a school, it's all locked in. Their grades and behavior are still being monitored. Consider taking CLEP tests in any subjects they're strong in. If they pass, they don't have to take (and don't have to pay for) the equivalent credits. Keep digging hard for grants and scholarships! Maybe take the SAT/ACT tests one more time. By late fall/winter, they should be pretty locked in and have applications in. The deadlines are usually by October or November, with decisions being made in December and January by the schools. Support them when opening those envelopes or emails, it can be crushing to be rejected. Maybe register for a prerequisite summer class at the local community college. They might get to liking it there, and it means a leg up on the journey.

Higher Education Years. By the time they go off to school, they're likely over eighteen years old, meaning it can lead them to apply for credit cards and loans without your knowledge or approval. Not much you can do about it! Hopefully, your lessons hold fast. If you're footing even part of the bill, require access to their grades and bursar account to monitor for things going sideways. They'll make a whole new set of friends, remind them about influences and their future. They don't have to actually go to class! Remind them that this is a requirement, and to be an adult, because they are one now.

Ask them to treat it like a job—show up on-time and be well prepared. The rest of their life depends on it. Be disciplined, create a schedule, put time in for fun. Be responsible on social media accounts. Find a quiet refuge to study (not the dorm or other loud places). They're so close, remind them to not blow it now. Adult actions have adult consequences, and the local/campus police typically have low tolerance for the stuff they have to deal with every day. They should have a job, on-campus or off. Check into work-study programs, internships, and other great opportunities that could lead them to immediate career employment upon graduation (or before!) Make sure they have a professional LinkedIn profile.

Another strategy to consider is working toward a December, rather than June, graduation. You are competing with far fewer graduates for those limited entry-level positions than you would be in June.

Case Study: My son was crestfallen when he received his decline from Penn State's main campus. It's a tough shot for a freshman. They accepted him at one of their smaller satellite campuses closer to home. He spent two years there, made lifelong friends, and got to play on the campus ice hockey team. Then he transferred to the main campus for junior/senior year, better prepared academically and by then was playing hockey at a level that allowed him to make the big team.

Case Study: My youngest daughter and I toured colleges in Maryland, Delaware, and our home state of Pennsylvania. She loved UDel, especially as it was near the beach, until I reminded her she'd be at home working during summers. As my wife was working at Hershey Medical Center, a teaching campus for Penn

State, we received a significant discount. We discussed with our daughter that we'd handle costs up to that price point if she went elsewhere, but she'd have to cover the rest herself. She made the wise, practical decision. However, the main campus was huge and intimidating to her, so she also went to a satellite campus for the first two years, then transferred for all that fun, tailgate action in Happy Valley.

Tax Notes

Track all education savings carefully. Make sure you know the nuances of the various tax breaks:

American Opportunity Tax Credit. Can be used for the first four years of undergraduate tuition, fees, books, supplies, equipment. You get 100% of the first $2,000 spent, 25% of the next $2,000, for a total annual credit of $2,500 for each student, as of this writing.

Lifetime Learning Credit. You get 20% of the first $10,000 for college tuition, fees, books for a total maximum credit of $2,000/year. This can be for graduate or undergraduate classes.

Tuition and Fees Tax Deduction. This one expired at the end of 2020, so keep an eye out in case it gets revived. You can't claim this the same year you use the above two, so use those first. This one allows eligible taxpayers to deduct up to $4,000 from taxable income to cover education costs.

Keep in mind that scholarships, grants, and GI Bill help are excluded from taxable income when used for qualified expenses.

If your employer helps out, you can exclude up to $5,250 of those benefits from taxable income, but must claim anything over that amount.

In closing, some other great resources are consumerfinance.gov/paying-for-college, bigfuture.collegeboard.org, studentaid.gov, and Anthony O'Neal's Debt Free Degree book.

CHAPTER TEN

Investing Part 1

FATTENING FROGS FOR SNAKES

"The Stock Market is designed to transfer money from the Active to the Patient."

Warren Buffett

W hat does "fattening frogs for snakes" in this chapter's sub-title mean? Well, for one, as a blues musician, it's one of my favorite songs, by the late, great Sonny Boy Williamson II. It's also an old-time saying that alludes to not putting a bunch of time, effort, or money into something that's only going to benefit others. And with investing, there are so many snakes, even legal ones. Fattening frogs for snakes is exactly what most people are inadvertently doing when they invest.

Why? Investing intimidates most people. They believe in the mirage that there's some special expertise other people have, and worth paying lots of money for. They're scared that if they do it themselves, they'll lose everything and end up working at Walmart in their 80s. That's all bull. Here are two important maxims to start this chapter with. I'll expand on each.

Investing done right is simple, and history proves that simple always wins over the long haul.

The fewer people and rules between you and your hard-earned money, the better.

Let's get started. We'll take it step-by-step. The key question is "Where should I put my money?" Let's tackle that first. Let's zoom out to the high-level and break the answer down into three of the most typical broad categories. We can get more into the weeds as you learn more. As a note, when I give the historical rate of return for cash, bonds, and stocks, it is the **nominal (before inflation) rate of return**. The rate of return after inflation is called the **real rate of return**.

Cash

Hey, you can just put it under the bed or bury it in the yard, right? The most skeptical, scared, risk intolerant among us might do that. It seems like the "safest" thing, because it's right there under you each night. But, fire, tornadoes/hurricanes, and burglars would like a word. Let's rule that option out. It's dumb. Some people hoard gold. That sounds like a sure way to put a target on your back when the stuff hits the fan and the apocalypse happens. People won't want bling, bartering will be all about guns, ammo, water, and food.

The average historical nominal return on cash is 1-2%, before inflation (and often negative when factoring it in). The go-to option for cash savings is the good old bank/credit union savings account. I'm a much bigger fan of credit unions than corporate banks, because they've always treated me better. When you're a member, you're an owner, after all. As you likely know, when you put money in a bank account, the bank pays you monthly interest—a percentage of your account balance. Free money! Some more than others, though, and we'll get to that.

The government insures legit banks/credit unions—the FDIC, to be specific. They cover each account up to $250,000. That means your money is very safe. What about that apocalypse? Hey, if that happens, we're all pretty screwed. A good practice is to have a checking account and linked savings account at a good credit union. I say "linked" because there are certain protections you can use, such as making sure if you overdraw your checking account, money is automatically transferred from your savings. Keep a healthy amount there to cover this case, but not too much. A thousand bucks should do it, plus some kind of buffer in your checking (typically $500). Overdraft fees are expensive, so avoid them. Your bank/credit union will normally remove them once or twice a year, so make that call and ask them to if it happens.

You should have a cash emergency fund of 3-6 months of your expenses. That shouldn't sit in the linked savings account we just discussed, because those rarely give the highest interest payments (but if they do, great, problem solved). I use and like ally.com because of their high interest payments, great customer service, and ability to create virtual savings accounts for things like vacations, holidays, cars without having to open a bunch of separate accounts. Your bank/credit union may have a money market account that gives a higher interest rate than their regular savings account with the same FDIC insurance.

You can also save cash in a brokerage account. What's that? As opposed to a bank/credit union, a brokerage is where stock trading and other types of transactions happen. We'll get to that.

For now, just recognize that a savings account in a brokerage is usually called a money market **fund**. Same deal as the bank/credit union's money market **account**, except no FDIC insurance on the fund. It's not a big concern, because these typically hold ultra-safe investments—US short-term treasuries.

Banks/credit unions are the safest, so why not put all your money there? Because of inflation. It sure feels good to check your balance and see your money sitting there all pretty. Like so many things with money, it's a mirage. The money is actually shrinking, because the cost of everything is going up, as it always does. That's called inflation. The money's there alright, but it just can't buy as much stuff. It's shrunk. A thousand bucks goes nowhere near as far as it did a hundred years ago!

I think we talked about cash enough, but to that last point, keep one important fact in mind. The more risk you're willing to take with your money, the more you are likely to make, and the bumpier (more volatile) the ride will be. But over time, you'll generally make more by taking more risk.

CDs and Laddering

You can buy certificates of deposit (CDs) at your bank or online. The idea here is that you fork over some cash for a certain period of time, and get it back with interest at the end of the term/contract. With money, the more risk you're willing to take, the more you can (potentially) receive over the long haul. But it also stands true that the longer you're willing to give someone your money to hold, the more they'll pay you. CDs are a good example of that. For example, you might get a one-year CD at 2% interest, a two-year CD at 2.5%, a three-year at 3%, a four year at 3.5%, and a five-year at 4%. Obviously, you want the best return, that 4%, but it stinks to have to lock the money up for five years. What if you need money in a year?

A solution would be to ladder. If you had $50,000, you might put $10,000 in each of those. Then, in one year when the paltry one-year CD matures, take the money and invest it in another five-year CD. If you do that for another four years, think about where that leaves you. You now have all five-year CDs with the top interest, and you now have the benefit of one maturing every year, so you have pretty liquid access to the money.

Bonds (Fixed Income)

Now you know the deal about cash. You may think you're ready to take a little more risk for a little more return. What's the next step up? Bonds, I say, young person. Bonds are the thing. You've probably heard of them, but most people don't really know what they are or how they work. Think of it this way: when you "buy" a bond, you're actually the bank now, and you're loaning your money out!

The average historical nominal return on bonds is 3-4%, but as you'll see, there are many kinds of bonds. We'll get into that. Let's talk about municipal bonds first and use those for a simple example. Suppose your little burgh of Mayberry wants to put in a new park system and pool, and it will cost a cool million bucks. They don't want to use their own cash reserves or borrow from the big banks. They may decide to issue municipal bonds to raise the money, and put out a notice—Mayberry Twp is offering 5-year municipal bonds at 3% interest! Maybe you're sitting there with too much money in a measly savings account and it's only earning 1%. That 3% bond sounds good—triple good! Note: A fancy name for the bond's interest rate is called its "coupon rate."

You pony up $10,000 and fork it over. You've loaned Mayberry Township $10k! They will now honor their commitment to pay you interest every six months until the bond matures in five years. Then you get your $10,000 back. If you need the $10k before the bond matures, you can't just ask for it back. It doesn't work that way. You made a deal! You can sell bonds on the open marketplace though. Suppose after three years, you want to sell the bond. But, what if interest rates have gone up, and people can buy a brand new bond at 4% interest return? Your 3% Mayberry bond wouldn't sell, right? To get a buyer, you'd have to discount it, maybe sell it for less than the $10,000 you paid/lent. Therefore, rising interest is bad for existing bonds (but good for new ones). There is an inverse relationship between bond prices and interest rates. Bonds have interest rate risk! You can mitigate that somewhat by buying shorter term/maturity bonds.

If interest rates had dropped to 2%, you could sell your $10,000 bond for more than the face value. You may think you've gamed the system if you're sitting on a bond with a sweet interest rate, because rates have dropped radically since you bought it. But if the bond is callable, the entity that you bought it from can simply return your principle and any interested owed and the deal is off. How rude! If you want to truly lock your rate in, get non-callable bonds. Most municipal and corporate bonds are callable. Here's a simple example—when you refinance your home mortgage for a lower interest rate, you have essentially called that loan from the bank. You paid them back and got a new loan at a cheaper rate.

Bonds have different maturities. Those that mature in one to three years are called short-term bonds. Four to ten years is an intermediate term. Anything longer is, well, long term. If interest rates were ultra low, as they were in 2020-2021, would you buy a 30-year bond? Heck no. As interest rates climbed in 2022 to fight inflation, people were buying short-term bonds, so that they'd expire quickly and they could buy new ones at the next highest interest rate. Long-term bonds pay higher interest than shorter-term bonds. You usually get paid more to lock up your money for longer, just like with bank certificates of deposit. You can ladder bonds just like CDs!

Don't confuse a bond's term or maturity with its duration. That's a common mistake. A bond's duration is a measure of its sensitivity to interest rates, based on its term, its coupon/interest rate, and whether it's callable. The higher the duration number, the more the bond's price may fall if interest rates rise. It's an important metric to observe if you're buying bonds to escape the volatility of the stock market.

Other kinds of bonds are United States Treasury bonds (same deal, only loaning the money to Uncle Sam rather than Mayberry Twp), and corporate bonds (you're loaning your money to companies). You can buy those US bonds directly on treasurydirect.gov, or at brokerages for no extra cost. The USA has never defaulted on a bond, so they're ultra-safe. It is incredibly rare for a municipality to default on a bond, so those are safe, too. In fact, those munis (as they're called) also have some tax advantages too. Of course, if you're buying corporate bonds, there's a higher risk of default. Companies go bankrupt sometimes!

Corporate bonds are rated on a scale from AAA to D. The higher the rating, the more secure the company and your bond are. A bond rated BB or below is considered a "junk bond." That's a nasty label, but is it terrible? Not necessarily. They're also called "high-yield, or non-investment grade bonds," which are much nicer (but misleading?) names. A bond may be rated that way because the company is fairly new and doesn't have a good enough borrowing track record yet. It could be the Starbucks of tomorrow! Remember earlier, when we said a basic rule of investing is the more risk you take, the more reward you experience? That holds true here. Lower-rated bonds like this pay more. It's all some people buy, because even here in the bond junkyard, the rates of default are pretty low.

I want to touch on one last problem with bonds. Remember that inflation thing we talked about earlier? And remember when you loaned out that $10k to Mayberry Twp, and got it back five years later? What if you'd bought the bond in 2021, when inflation was rock-bottom low? During 2022 and 2023 (as of this writing!) inflation was rising fast. When you get your $10k back from Mayberry five years later, if there's been high inflation, it's not really worth as much, is it? Dang, it shrunk. That can be a problem, which is why you can buy bonds that are inflation protected. You pay a small premium for the benefit of having your bond principal adjusted regularly for inflation. It would be a good idea in years like 2021, when inflation had nowhere to go but up!

Stocks (Equities)

Everybody climb on board the roller coaster and buckle up! Bring your purses and wallets! Here's where the ride becomes wild. No more boring cash and bonds in this neighborhood. Remember, we said when buying bonds you are *loaning*? Well, when you buy stocks, you are *owning*! That's right, sports fans. If you log into a trading platform such as Vanguard, Fidelity, Ally, or others, and buy a share of Starbucks stock, you are part-owner of the company. Strut on in there, demand a free latte, and start bossing your employees around (good luck!). The average historical nominal rate of return on stocks is 8-10%.

OK, while you may not get bossing-around privileges, you may now share in the gains (and losses) of the company. There are two primary ways to make money from your share of the company. The first one is when, each quarter, the company reviews its profits/losses and decides whether to share any profits with its shareholders. If they do, this payment is called a dividend. Big, established companies pay dividends each quarter (every three months), like clockwork. Smaller companies may not pay dividends for a long time, preferring instead to invest those profits into growing the company more. That leads us to the second way to make money from your share ownership. Suppose you bought that share of Starbucks a while back, when they were $80 each. Currently, the shares are worth over $100. You could sell your share and make a $20 profit.

When the stock market is on a roll, it's called a bull market. When it's on a slide, that's called a bear market. Up years are far more typical than down years, and over time, despite the volatility, the market has only gone up and up. But it's a bumpy ride. Don't let your emotions cause bad decisions. For example, many investors sold all their shares when the market was dropping rapidly in the 2008 financial crisis. They lost a ton of money by taking those losses, selling already-devalued shares, and missed the rebound over the following years that would have rewarded them with 6x growth in share value, plus all the dividends paid over that time, even when it was down.

Buy low, sell high. Buy and hold for the win. Invest consistently (called dollar cost averaging). If you invest just $150/month starting at age twenty, fifty years later at a conservative 8% rate of return, you'd be a millionaire at age seventy! If you wait until you're fifty to invest, you'd have to put $1,800/month away to hit that million at age seventy, rather than that measly $150. Too many people live for the moment, and sacrifice the best years of their lives, relegating their older years to greeting shoppers at Walmart or sitting at home rather than exploring the world.

You might ask, "If stocks are so great, why wouldn't I just put all my money there?" The thing about the stock market, compared to interest rates and bond prices, is that it's a much more volatile and wild ride. Any hiccup in world or economic events can send stock prices tumbling or through the roof. For that reason, it's unwise to put money there that you may need within the next few years. If your home down payment money is in the market, and something like COVID happens right before you're supposed to close, your $80k may turn into $60k within one or two days, and now you may not have your 10% down on the house.

Imagine you just hit your retirement goal of $1,000,000, knowing you can pay your bills with a safe withdrawal rate of 4%, or $40,000/year (in addition to Social Security, pensions, etc). If the money is all in stocks, and a big market decline happens right after you retire, you're in trouble. Your million dollars may now be only $700,000, and your $40,000 annual withdrawal has gone from a safe 4% rate to an unsafe 6% rate. You may well run out of money! This situation is called sequence of returns risk, where you depend on stocks, and forced to sell shares while they're down. We'll talk about ways to avoid that in the retirement chapter.

Who loses money in the stock market?

- People who panic sell in a down market

- People who try to time the market—"I'll buy when it starts going up!"

- People who invest money they'll need in the short term

- People who try to pick winners and losers in single stocks and don't rely on diversity

- People who day trade, buy based on "tips," buy into investments with expensive commissions/fees, or pay advisors too much

That said, if you lose money on your investments in a brokerage (non-retirement) account, it's a tax write-off. And listen, when you log in and see your account balance is way down because of a stock market drop, *you haven't lost money!* The *value* of your assets has been temporarily lowered. The stock market has never failed to rebound, and rebound big. Those people who freaked during 2008-2009 and went to cash missed out on the recovery that followed. Is that guaranteed? Nope. But it's never failed to happen. Again, you only really lose the money when you sell low. Then you've locked in those losses. Buy low, sell high. Savvy investors see a down market as a big sale, and act accordingly.

Use the guidance I'm providing to position yourself such that what the stock market is doing doesn't matter. It only matters if shares you need to sell are suddenly devalued, right? Don't put yourself in that position. Savvy investors actually love it when the market is down, and everyone else is losing their stuff over it. Why? Because they're dollar cost averaging and have their dividend distributions set to reinvest automatically. They know they're getting new dividend-producing shares "on sale." We all love a good, legit sale, don't we?

Income vs Growth vs Value, Oh My

You may often hear the terms growth stocks, income stocks, value stocks. If you peruse a list of funds available in your brokerage account or retirement plan at work, you'll likely see choices with those names. We'll get into what funds are in a moment, but let's clear up what these terms mean first.

When we talked about the big, established companies that regularly pay dividends, we were talking about **income stocks.** They're referred to that way because traditionally, retirees like those, because, drumroll please, the consistent dividend payments create an income stream. The smaller companies that may not pay dividends, because they're trying to grow more quickly, are called **growth stocks**. Because these companies are typically new and growing, the real bargain here is the growth in the share price. It tends to be better than dividends, but it's riskier. Remember our adage, more risk, more reward. These companies could be the Google or Amazon of tomorrow! **Value stocks** are simply companies whose shares are considered by the experts to be selling for below their real value. For example, a scandal hit when the CEO was found to be embezzling company funds and the share price took a dive, but now the board of directors has hired a bright new promising CEO. Which kind is best to have? All of them! Remember, diversity always wins over the long haul. Trying to pick winners and losers, well, loses.

What's a Stock Index?

You often hear the term "stock market" but what is that, exactly? It's what it sounds like—a marketplace to buy stocks. Of course, the New York Stock Exchange on Wall Street is such a place, but these days most people do so online. When you hear "the stock market is up" or "the stock market is down" there is usually a graphic of what's happening in the Dow Jones Industrial Average (DJIA), or "Dow Index." So, what's *that*, then? It's a stock index, which is a hypothetical, virtual grouping of companies. For example, the Dow/DJIA is a grouping of just thirty monster-sized industrial companies like Coca-Cola, 3M, and Chevron. Just thirty companies, that's not diverse, and certainly not representative of all 4,000 or so publicly traded companies in the United States!

You often hear about the S&P 500 Index. That's a similar hypothetical grouping of companies, only this time it's the five hundred largest companies in the US stock market. Ok, that's more diverse than the Dow! But, it's still a lot of those big, income type companies. You hear big companies referred to as "large cap" which means their capitalization/net worth is, well, large. Mid-caps are middle-sized companies, and small caps are those smaller growth oriented companies we talked about. There are indexes that group small cap stocks together, like the Russell 2000, and tech companies (NASDAQ). Doing this makes it easier for analysts or regular people to see how a particular sector is doing at any moment.

Single Stocks

You wonder how you would know what companies to buy. That's easy! The answer is, "All of them." As Jack Bogle says, "Why search for a needle in the haystack when you can buy the whole haystack?" Before I show you how, let me explain why it's not good to buy single company stocks, at least for your important goals. You might think the company is great, because in your profession and role as an expert, you use their products and love them. Even if that's the case, you do not know what's going on inside that company or its competitors. An announcement could be imminent that their flagship product causes cancer, or their CEO has been embezzling, or their competitor is about to release a better product for free or at a lower cost. Let's look at some examples.

At the dawn of the COVID pandemic, Zoom seemed like a slam dunk to buy. Everybody will go to school and work remotely, right? Can't miss! It'll be selling like hotcakes. And it did for a bit, until a huge security hole allowed people to randomly jump on Zoom meetings and do gross things. Whoops, the stock took a dive. Ok, they fixed that, shares started to recover, then boom, Google announces their free Meet tool, which basically does the same thing as Zoom, but for free (that's what I use!). Zoom shares took a dive again. Then, they recovered, and vaccines were announced, and they dropped again. Ya never know!

Same with Peloton—gyms were closed, people had to exercise at home during the pandemic. Sure thing, right? Yes, until their treadmill product was involved in a child's death and a massive recall occurred.

How about Enron, the energy company that was the darling of Wall Street and considered a sure thing? Or Luckin Coffee, which all the buzz had as being the next Starbucks. People invested fortunes in those stocks and lost it all when massive fraud was uncovered. They cooked the books. Those amazing numbers were all fraudulent.

If you want to invest in single stocks, do it in a side brokerage account and only with your fun money. There's nothing wrong with it as a hobby if that's what you're into, same as with playing blackjack, bingo, poker, scratch-offs. As long as it's money you're prepared to lose and it won't affect your important goals and needs.

Fun with Funds

So, what's the alternative to buying single stocks? Buying baskets of them! Let's look at an example. It's public knowledge which five hundred companies are in the S&P 500 index. In your retirement fund choices, you probably see an S&P 500 index fund as one of them. Instead of having to build your own diversity by purchasing shares of all those companies, the index fund makes it easy. It contains shares of all those companies in one basket, so you just buy shares of the fund itself and you own them all.

What if you wanted total diversity—all four thousand publicly traded stocks? This would be a great idea, because with an S&P 500 fund, you aren't getting those great small growth stocks. Therefore, some investors will instead buy a total US stock market index fund, such as Vanguard's VTSAX, the largest fund in the world. Many people buy it for that reason. It's easy diversification. It's that haystack that Jack Bogle was talking about when he said not to look for the needle, just buy the whole haystack.

These funds that group stocks together are commonly called mutual funds. They're not all "index" funds, because not all of them track indexes. For example, you might be into healthcare stocks, but not want to pick individual winners and losers. You can easily find and invest in specific mutual funds for industry sectors like healthcare, construction, tech, and many others. But, wait a minute—it's easy to build an S&P 500 fund. We just search on what companies are in that index and that's the recipe. How do the companies in a healthcare fund get chosen? You'd want only the best ones, and not the stinkers, right?

These funds are called actively managed funds. They need managers. If Fidelity is going to create a healthcare mutual fund to offer to its customers, it's got to find some folks that are not only healthcare industry experts but also financial experts, to manage the fund and make those in or out decisions daily. As you can guess, since they're the world's top experts in not one but two fields, the fund managers get paid big bucks! Who pays for them? The fund owners.

Funds have expenses associated with them, mostly to pay the fund managers, but also for trading and admin expenses. The simple, easy decision S&P 500 fund doesn't need managers, so the expenses on them (called an "expense ratio") is usually extremely low, such as .05% (that's five hundredths of a percent!). It's a passive fund, no managers needed. Active funds have higher expenses associated with them, of course, usually upwards of 1% or more. It doesn't sound like a lot, but it is, and really creates a drag on your investment returns over time. Hey, if you buy a total US stock market fund, you have all those great healthcare companies, and the tech, and so on. When someone brags that their Tesla or Apple shares are up, just yawn, draw a check-mark in the air, and say, "Yeah, I own that."

Mutual funds are great. There is one problem, though. Suppose your granny left you $100k out of the blue, and you wake up the next morning and see the market is down at the opening. What a great time to buy—buy low! So you eagerly log in and buy $100k of VTSAX at 9:30am when the price is showing as say, $80/share. The next day you see your transaction verification and it says you bought at $100/share. What? The reason is that mutual fund purchases happen after market close, not "in the moment" like regular single stock share purchases. Apparently, the market had a big rally during the day, and you paid way more than you expected to.

A newer type of mutual fund called Exchange Traded Funds (ETFs) solves this problem. They're mutual funds, but they trade just like single stocks. If you get in your time machine and go back a day, you can then buy Vanguard VTI instead, which is the ETF version of VTSAX. It's the same bunch of jelly beans (total US stock market), just in a different container. ETFs also have lower expense ratios and some tax efficiencies. They're all the rage these days! Of course, for dollar-cost-averaging type purchases, automatic over time like your retirement plan contributions at work, this doesn't matter much. So you might not see ETF choices there.

Bond Funds

Now that we know what funds are, let's skip back to our bonds topic. You can buy bond funds as well. Instead of buying US treasury bonds directly on treasurydirect.gov, you can buy funds that hold short, intermediate, or long-term US treasuries. You can buy bond funds that only hold municipal bonds, real estate bonds, or corporate bonds. A go-to for many people, again for maximum diversity, is an aggregate bond fund. Those track an index called the Barclay's bond index and contain all the above types of bonds.

We mentioned earlier that bonds act like a great shock absorber in a portfolio, because when the stock market is down, bond funds usually go up. That's called an inverse correlation. But aggregate bonds funds aren't as inverse as, say, US treasuries, because aggregate funds have those corporate bonds. However, also because they have the higher yielding corporate bonds, they do usually return more money. Pick your poison. Younger folks like the aggregate returns, risk averse retirees like the certainty and inverse behavior of US treasuries, and often with the TIPS inflation protection. Earlier, we discussed laddering bonds with different maturities. That's a bit of work, but now there are laddered bond ETFs that make this easier.

Alternatives/Commodities/Real Estate

When times are bad, you often also hear the screaming to run to gold, or silver, or some other alternative investment. Yes, metals do rise when the stock market dives, as a place of refuge for some. The problem is that after the scare is over and the market settles, these types of investments go right back where they were. They don't have a rising value over time, more like an EKG graph of your heartbeat. They also don't pay dividends.

Real estate is a different matter. You can buy in easily with a simple real estate investment trust (REIT) ETF like Vanguard's VNQ. If you want to get into house flipping, or buying properties to rent, go slow at first. This sounds great, but being a landlord isn't for everyone. Make sure you know the business and market inside and out, because your competition will, and they'll be far more experienced than you. Mistakes are expensive! Read my book *Show and Sell 2023* for tons of tips. That said, aggregate bond funds have real estate exposure through holding mortgage-backed securities.

Key Takeaways (So Far)

This is a long chapter, by necessity. Let's take a breath here and cover some of the main bullet points so far.

- The long-term average return on cash is 1-2%, bonds 3-4%, and stocks 8-10%.

- Don't put money into stocks that you'll need in the near future (less than 5-10 years).

- Don't try to time the market—invest regularly and consistently. Don't act on tips.

- Avoid fees, expenses, and having your money locked up.

- Don't panic sell in a down market. Buy and hold, buy low and sell high.

- The fewer people and rules between you and your money, the better.

- Avoid managed/active funds and focus on inexpensive, simple index funds.

"Don't look for the needle in the haystack. Just buy the haystack."

Jack Bogle

CHAPTER ELEVEN

Investing Part 2

"Only when the tide goes out do you discover who's been swimming naked."

Warren Buffett

Asset Allocation

Asset allocation is how your assets are allocated! Duh. Ok, well, specifically, it's used regarding your liquid assets (your money), not your physical assets like your house and cars. Asset allocation is typically stated as something like "60/40." The numbers correlate to how much of your nest egg is in equities (stocks), and fixed income (bonds and cash). Sometimes, the fixed income part is separate, like 60/30/10 for stocks/bonds/cash.

Why is this important? We discussed earlier that it would be bad to have a portfolio that's very heavy in stocks just prior to entering retirement, when you would need that money. If some sixty-five-year-old dude tells you he's 90/10 and ready to retire, that should give you pause. Same thing if the dude says he's 10/90! So, what's the right mix? Ah, that recipe is part of the secret sauce. It depends.

Your asset allocation should be a function of your personal degree of risk tolerance, your time horizon to needing the money, and your income needs. Someone young and at the start of their career should be at a more aggressive asset allocation for retirement money, such as 90/10 or 80/20. Retirees typically enter retirement at something between 60/40 or 50/50. This means your asset allocation should be on a managed glide path toward being more conservative as you approach the time you'll start using the money. Same thing for 529 college savings plan investments.

In fact, most brokerages offer "target date" retirement funds. If you're a 30-year-old in 2025 who wants to retire at age sixty in 2055, that target date fund is likely sitting at an 80/20 asset allocation, or thereabouts, in 2025. The fund managers (oh, those people again...) will manage the glide path for you, year by year, to make sure it's a comfortable 50/50 or so by the year 2055. We'll discuss this more in the chapter on retirement planning.

I mentioned your natural, DNA-based, built-in risk tolerance level as an ingredient for your asset allocation recipe. Everyone is different. Some people get scared by roller coasters, others love the thrill. Some of those roller coaster lovers would never scuba dive. Many scuba divers would never jump out of an airplane with a parachute. It's all relative, but it's important.

We said this book is about happiness, not money. If you're naturally very risk averse, but you have invested aggressively, you're going to be stressed and upset every time the stock market takes a dip or dive. Often, spouses/partners are opposites! This is usually a big part of all the fighting that goes on about money between couples. It's the number one cause of relationship stress and breakups, after all. It's important to understand this about each other, and come to a happy medium together. There are quizzes out there that will help you each score your risk tolerance level. That said, you should always run the numbers (or have an advice-only unbiased advisor like me do it for you) to make sure that your 'comfortable' asset allocation will also meet your money needs in the future.

I'm all for simple, inexpensive, easy-to-understand investment portfolios. The numbers show nothing beats them over the course of time. With what you've learned so far, if you've determined you're comfortable with a 75/25 asset allocation, and it meets your financial needs, you could simply take 75% of your money and buy a total US stock market ETF and spend the other 25% on an aggregate bond fund ETF and poof, you're done! How easy is that!?

Diversity is important, though. I keep saying that. The Vanguard Boglehead disciples are advocates of a three-fund portfolio. That means you should diversify your stock portion just a bit more—to include those great international companies like Toyota, Nestle, Alibaba, and others. How do we change our investing recipe to accommodate that? You could take that 75% in stock and split it between the total US stock market ETF and a total international (minus, or ex-US) ETF. Vanguard currently recommends slightly less than half your stocks be in international, although this guidance is always changing based on world economic forecasts. Be cautious of the term 'world' in these fund names, and 'international'. World funds usually include US stocks, whereas international (ex-US) funds do not.

What this all boils down to is that investing done right is booooring! You figure out your asset allocation, asset location, set your portfolio up that way, then just check in annually at the start of the year and rebalance if market moves made it out of whack. That's the simple secret of investing. Nobody beats the market over time, so just invest in the market and find something else to do with your time. Set it and forget it. If you like to dabble, set up a fun money brokerage account and have fun. It's no different from people that like poker, blackjack, bingo, or playing the lottery for fun. Just make sure it's under your entertainment budget and don't spend more than that.

Evaluating Funds

I use Vanguard in my examples, but there are plenty of similar choices elsewhere. Fidelity and Schwab are two other popular, lower-cost brokerages. They both have ETF and regular mutual fund choices similar to Vanguard's. If you have an account at any of those, you can buy Vanguard funds, or any of the others. It's a pretty wide open market! The only time your choices are limited, typically, are in your retirement plan choices at work. We'll get to that in the chapter on retirement planning.

Vanguard was created by a humble man, Jack Bogle, who wanted a brokerage for working people. Bogle came from a family that lost everything, including their home, in the Great Depression. His parents divorced. He persevered, and vowed to make investing available to everyone, not just the wealthy. Bogle invented the index fund, and advocated for low-fee, simple, patient investing. He's a hero of mine, and that's why I do things the same way. Because it's the only thing that's ever worked over the long haul. When you buy shares in a Vanguard fund, you are an owner of that fund, sort of a credit union model. They're a company that actually picks up the phone when you call, and they're patient and clear in their advice.

How do you know a fund is good? I like to use morningstar .com. It's free for regular folks. They'll pitch you with a pop-up for the paid upgrade, but all you need is in the free resources. I'll search for a fund and look for a few key pieces of information. First is the Morningstar rating, based on a five-star scale. Don't put a huge amount of stock in this though, it's often based on past (not projected) performance. So, coming out of a period of very low inflation, you might see an inflation-protected bond fund with a low rating. But if you know you're in times like these, as I currently write, where inflation is rising, it might still be a great strategic choice.

On the Quote tab at Morningstar, I check the expense ratio. This is the aforementioned fees you pay the fund managers and other expenses in the fund. Anything over half a percent (.5%) is high, in my opinion. If you decide you're just going to set it and forget it with a target date retirement fund, something below a half a percent isn't bad. You're paying someone to manage that glide path for you. The funds I usually recommend to clients, such as the Vanguard ETF funds, have expense ratios around .05%. That's ridiculously low! Every dollar is going to *you*, not active fund managers and other fees.

On this same tab, Morningstar states whether the fee level is average, below average, above average for this type of fund. It also says whether there are loads (commissions) on the fund. Avoid those! They show the time-to-market (TTM, or lifetime) yield, too. That's about how much the fund will make you, percentage-wise, each year. It shows the turnover rate. That's a measure of how much trading is going on inside the fund. Actively managed funds can have high turnover, which could mean high taxes for you if it's in a brokerage account.

I flip to the Risk tab next. It shows me a nice thumbnail of how much risk versus return this fund has compared to others in its category. Next up is the Portfolio tab. This shows me the asset allocation within the fund, in terms of how much US equity, international equity, fixed income, cash, etc. Scroll further down and you can see the biggest holdings in the fund (what companies it's invested in).

A great hack is to look up some example target date funds for the year you plan to retire, and see exactly how the best and brightest minds at Vanguard, Fidelity, and other brokerages choose to invest for people retiring in that year. You can then build that same portfolio yourself and save the expenses! You only have to remember to manage the glide path, and make it slowly more conservative as you move toward retirement. Same goes for college savings, by looking at their 529 plan fund investments.

Investment Advisors

Hey, that's me! Do you need one? Probably not. D'oh, I just fired myself! In reality, I mostly work with do-it-yourself people who just want a second set of eyes or advice on what they're doing, or are too busy to do it all themselves. It's money well spent—I often catch mistakes or find optimizations that pay for my fees many times over. That's what a good investment advisor does. I don't manage other people's money. I believe they should do it themselves, as it's not hard. Remember, the fewer people and rules between you and your money, the better. I practice what I preach. I mostly do financial/retirement/FIRE planning, which is fun and a bit more complex than most folks can handle, due to all the moving parts. But I teach folks as I go, so they can take the wheel if they want.

Be very careful—some people that call themselves "advisors" are just salespeople, who will always "advise" you to buy their products. They get paid commission, which means they aren't really fiduciaries obligated to do the best thing for you. They'll sell you whatever makes them wealthier. It's sad they can even use those titles, and they're truly wolves in sheep's clothing. It only takes a free steak dinner, or "free" one-hour meeting with the wrong person to undo a lifetime of hard work and damage your retirement.

That's me. What do most other advisors do? They'll offer you a free financial plan, or steak dinner, to lure you into either buying an expensive, complex insurance/investing product, or to get you to turn your entire nest egg over to them to manage, or both. Most advisors who manage client investments charge around one percent. Let's do that math. If you have $500,000 invested with them, you're paying $5,000 a year, or about $417/month. For doing what? If they're doing it right, as you can see from what you learned, they're not doing a lot of work. And as your money grows, as it always does when invested well, you pay more and more for that same amount of non-work.

It boils down to the more you have, the more they charge for the same amount of work. If you have a million, that per-month is now over $800. Wow! That's a nice car payment. To me, this is against the fiduciary obligation. Charging more for the same work is not in the client's best interest. You never see those fees because they come out of your investment portfolio. And worse, if they're doing this wrong, wheeling and dealing, trying to pick winners and losers with your money, you stand to lose a lot more. So many advisors won't even work with people with less than $500,000 to invest, pushing aside regular working folks who really need the help most.

Our pension funds here in Pennsylvania, like many, are struggling. A new governor took over and had them looked at. His study determined that it was because the fund managers were doing exactly this—trying to pick winners and losers. What fun, gambling with other people's money! The determination was that if they had just invested it exactly as I've described, in boring old index funds, the pensions would be solvent and more.

Warren Buffett did a similar experiment in 2008, when he invested a million dollars in an index fund and compared it to the best hedge fund returns every year. Warren recommends in his will that the money he leaves behind to his heirs be invested in index funds and short-term bonds. I'm dropping the mic here. The guy is the most brilliant investor of our time, maybe ever. It's also the philosophy of Jack Bogle. He started Vanguard based on low costs and ethics, as there were no brokerages for working people at the time. Anyway, this happens again and again with pension funds, not to mention individual advisors or advisory firms—particularly the big ones you see lots of commercials for. You know the ones who promise that when you do better, they do better. Uh-huh.

Some advisors also get paid by "recommending" or just going ahead and investing you in the funds they get paid commissions/loads on. I've seen it many times. Client hands over their nest egg, and it's immediately given a 5.75% (wow!) haircut as the advisor buys funds and gets paid that big commission. The loss of return on that money over your lifetime is incredible. Advisors who don't get commissions call themselves "fee-only," but be careful. The term has been co-opted and may not always mean that. There are similar names, like fee-based and fee-offset, that confuse people. Those latter two mean the advisor charges for their time, but also gets commissions.

It's not a bad thing to hire an advisor who has the heart of a teacher, and will show you the ropes or give you an annual check-up to make sure you're on track and not making mistakes. Look for someone that's advice-only, flat-fee, fee-only, and fiduciary. Look them up on adviserinfo.sec.gov or brokercheck.finra.org and see if there are any discrepancies or disclosures on their record. Download and read through their advisor disclosure (ADV) form. Check any Google and Yelp ratings.

I'm an Accredited Financial Counselor, an AFC®, which I believe is a higher standard than CFP®, because it requires expertise in all of personal finance, not just "planning." It's an organization that's based on true altruism, caring about people, rather than world dominance and profit. You'll see lots of commercials touting the trustworthiness of those bearing the CFP® mark, but the reality is much darker. They rely on advisors that have done bad things to self-report those disclosures, crimes, violations, etc. How's that going? See the blog post on my website for the deets.

Another good option, if you'd like some guidance on the cheap, is Vanguard's Personal Advisor Service, which charges a low 0.3% for their investing advice. They won't get into all the nuances of retirement or financial planning like I do, but they're solid on the investing front. Spoiler alert—they'll tell you to invest just as I am in this chapter.

If you're going to work with someone, ask good questions:

- How do you charge? What are *all* your fees? Do you use complicated, expensive fee structures for managing my assets (AUM) that charge you more just because I have more?

- Is your 'free' retirement/financial plan used in order to lure you into the above? Is it only free if I agree to let you manage my assets?

- Do you sell insurance? People that call themselves mis-leading names (counselor, coach, associate, etc) often aren't real advisors. Many are insurance people trying to sell you very complex, expensive annuities, perma-nent/cash-value life insurance, and other products.

- Are you a representative or registered as a broker-dealer? If so, the whole "fiduciary" thing becomes a big gray area.

Roboadvisors

Companies like Betterment use roboadvisors to do your investing. These are algorithms, and a kind of in-between choice between doing it yourself and hiring an advisor. They cost less than a human advisor, and often you have the option to consult with one if you feel you need to. Roboadvisors can do tax moves like harvesting for you on-the-fly. It seems scary to be trusting your nest egg to an algorithm, but they have a good track record (so far). I'm more of an old-school fan of doing it yourself and having all that power and knowledge. It's not that hard.

Gamified/Appified Investing

Technology invades every aspect of our lives, and investing is no different. Apps like Robin Hood, Think or Swim gamify the con-cept, and attempt to make it more fun and visual. They also add to the cost, and can cause a heavy price if they're tempting you to do more than you should. There are plenty of examples of that so far. I'd avoid them, and stick with the security and safety of the big houses for now.

Investing Fads and Trends

If you follow personal finance topics on social media, you'll see all the latest miracle techniques pitched, along with expensive classes to enrich the pitchers. For example, there's a whole segment that believes the correct approach to FI/investing is to buy up carefully selected dividend-paying single company stocks. Sigh. Yo, investing bro, Kodak and RadioShack used to pay great dividends! Where are they now? In the dustbin of big-dividend payer history, that's where, I tell ya. It's a bad idea for all the reasons we've discussed. You're pouring tons of money into companies that could disappear in a flash, along with their dividend payments. Those dividends aren't promised—companies can cut them off in a heartbeat, and they will if they need to. Too much exposure to equities exposes you to sequence risk (see the retirement chapter). Be diverse, you'll get great dividend payments (and growth, and value...).

There's another trend flying around that says traditional/Roth retirement plan funding is dumb old people's stuff, and you should instead put your money into Maximum Premium Indexing (MPI) which is incredibly risky for all the reasons I've stated about insurance products. It's just an indexed universal life (IUL) policy with a fancy new name (because we know all about IULs and why they're bad).

As far as crypto, sorry, it's still the wild west. There's too little oversight, and too much hacking risk. Hackers steal billions of crypto each year. The very best in the world in Russia, Iran, North Korea, China, and yup, right here in the U S of A have a very vested interest in your accounts. If you forget your password, it's gone anyway.

People who care about environment and social issues are tempted to invest in Environmental, Social, and Governance (ESG) funds. Those are funds that are supposed to avoid investing in things like fossil fuels and anything that's to the detriment of the ESG cause. To date, it hasn't worked out well, with the funds more name than substance. My preferred approach is to invest well, and take any profit/yield from undesirable sources and include it in my monthly contributions to the causes I care about.

Do you want to risk your hard-earned money on some new untested fad/method, or what has worked over the course of history in every kind of economy?

Investing and Taxes

You don't have to worry about making moves and changing your investments around in your retirement accounts (Roth and traditional) as far as taxes are concerned. You've already paid the taxes on the Roth accounts (just be sure not to take any gains out until you're eligible—only take your contributions if you have to withdraw prior to that). You get taxed on anything you take from the traditional accounts when you withdraw the money. It's taxed as straight income, same as your earned income, such as salary. So, those are easy tax-wise. It's your brokerage account you have to be careful with! The next chapter will go into more detail on taxes, and our retirement chapter will discuss Roth and traditional accounts.

Investing Summary

Ok, so here are the basic steps to investing success:

1. Figure out your risk tolerance, use it to determine your asset allocation.

2. Create an account (Vanguard, Fidelity, Schwab).

3. Buy the equity portion of the asset allocation in a total US market fund/ETF and total international fund/ETF.

4. Buy the bond portion in a total bond fund/ETF or intermediate-term US Treasuries or TIPS.

5. Adjust annually to ensure the asset allocation stays the same (or set it to do so automatically).

Pretty simple, right? Let's get to the advanced stuff, if you're up for it!

CHAPTER TWELVE

Advanced Investing/Taxes

HARVESTING, CONVERSIONS, OH MY!

"Buy when everyone else is selling and hold until everyone else is buying. That's not just a catchy slogan. It's the very essence of successful investing."

J. Paul Getty

Income Taxes

Let's fire off this chapter with an overview of how our progressive federal income tax system works here in the good old US of A. This is based on the tax brackets in 2023, which may have changed for later years by the time you read this. But, the flow and concept are the same.

Suppose you're single and made $100,000 gross income in 2023. But, you also contributed $10,000 to your company 401k or other pretax traditional retirement plan. That $10k comes right off your taxable income for the year, which is now $90k. You'll get taxed on the other $10k when you withdraw it in retirement. The company matched you 50%, so they put in $5,000, which has no impact on your taxable income for this example year.

Right-O. Now you're down to $90k taxable income. You notice that you're eligible to do an annual IRA contribution, so you send $5,000 from your checking account over to your IRA. That also comes off your taxable income, which is now down to $85k.

Right off the bat, you see that as a single filer; you get a sweet $13,850 standard deduction. We're assuming that, like most people, you don't have enough deductions to itemize. We take that standard deduction off your taxable income, $85k–$13,850 leaves $71,150 of the remaining taxable income. You haven't paid a penny yet!

Now we work our way through the brackets. The first one is the 10% bracket, which is good for up to $11,000. So we lop off $11k from your remaining $71,150, pay 10% tax on it, which is $1,100 due in federal income tax. Your remaining taxable income is now $60,150.

The second bracket is the 12% bracket. It's good for the amount between $11,000 (top of the 10% bracket) and $44,725, which is $33,725 worth of income. We tax that at 12% and get a tax bill of $4,047 on that section. Add the $1,100 owed from the 10% bracket and now you owe $5,147 in federal income tax, and have $26,425 left to tax.

The third bracket is the 22% bracket, which is for incomes above that $44,725 threshold and up to $95,375. Thus, it contains $50,650 worth of income between those two amounts. Well, we only have $26,425 left, so we tax that at 22%, which is $5,814. Add that to our prior tax due of $5,147 and we get $10,961 due in federal taxes for 2023. You have no more taxable income. A graph of this breakout is below.

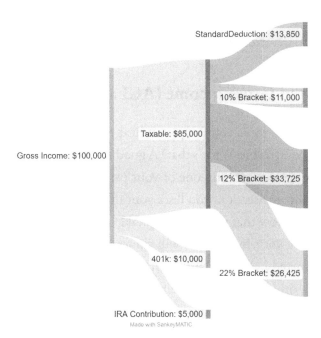

Now you look at your W2 form and see that your employer withheld $12,000 in federal income taxes from your paycheck over the year. Yay! You get a $1,039 refund! There are two important terms to know from this example. Your *marginal* tax rate is 22%. That's the term for the highest bracket you crept up into. Your *effective* tax rate is 15.4%, determined by dividing your $71,150 of taxable income (after the standard deduction, IRA contribution, 401k contributions) by your $10,961 of taxes owed.

This was a simple example to get folks to understand how our progressive tax system works. I've heard too many people say things like, "I don't want that bonus this year. It will cause me to move into the 22% bracket and my whole year of income will be taxed at that rate!" Not true, as you've seen. Take the dang bonus and celebrate.

Of course, other things factor into your income tax, such as interest payments from your bank or brokerage accounts. You may be eligible for some above-the-line deductions even if you don't qualify to itemize your deductions.

Adjusted Gross Income (AGI and MAGI)

When the tax topic comes up, you hear the term "adjusted gross income" quite a bit. What's that? A good way to follow along with this chapter is to pull up one of your prior year tax returns. Under the Income section, you'll see your income sources tallied up. You'll see below that where any capital losses can be stated, which will reduce your income. So will alimony payments for divorces that occurred before 2019, educator expenses, HSA deductions, and a few other things. The result after all this is your adjusted gross income (AGI). Your standard or itemized deductions are taken from this number as one of the steps to get to your ending tax owed for the year.

Modified Adjusted Gross Income (MAGI). The MAGI takes your AGI and adds certain things back in! Confused yet? Ugh, taxes. For most people, the AGI is the same as the MAGI. Interest that's normally tax-free, like municipal bond interest, is an example of something that gets added back in to AGI to get to the MAGI. The MAGI is used for things like calculating Affordable Care Act subsidies and how much you can contribute to a Roth account each year. In fact, some of the calculations use different variations of the MAGI.

Roth Conversions

Note: Always be clear whether you're talking about **conversions** versus **contributions**. IRA contributions are when you directly contribute money into the traditional or Roth IRA account. This commonly happens when taxes are done, because that's when you know if and how much you're allowed to contribute for the year. It's limited by your earned income, and the ranges are different for traditional and Roth contributions. You may be ineligible to make a traditional contribution for the year, but you may still be eligible to make a Roth contribution. In this section, we're going to talk about conversions, since those are more complex than simple contributions.

An important takeaway from the above tax lesson is the remaining space we saw in the 22% bracket. Remember, we said it covered up to $50,650 of income, but you only had $26,425 left to tax? That means there was $24,425 left of space (or headroom) in that 22% bracket. That's an excellent opportunity to do a Roth conversion, if you have money in a traditional IRA. You can do this without paying the 10% early withdrawal penalty if you are under age 59 1/2. In general, conversions at 12% tax rate and below are great, they're rarely done at over 30%, and the 22% and 24% are in the "it depends" zone, as we'll discuss.

In that case, you'd have to do all this analysis before the end of the year, because Roth conversions must be done by December 31. But how do you know all this if the year isn't over yet? This is why we get very busy with clients in early December. We have them pull together their most recent (maybe final) paystubs, statements, and use a fancy tax tool to figure it out. Roth conversions involve taking the money out of your pretax traditional IRA, intentionally paying the taxes on it, and then sticking it into a Roth IRA, where it will grow tax free for the rest of your life. This will also minimize your requirements to take required minimum distributions (RMDs) in your 70s and keep your taxes lower late in life. They're a beautiful thing! But, don't pay the taxes due out of the conversion money. Those dollars are precious, you want them going into the Roth. Pay the taxes out of pocket when you file your taxes. Here, it would be $24,425 X 22% = $5,330. Have that money on hand to pay when you file.

You can do Roth conversions at any point during the year, but there's some risk in that. What if you **plan** to be in the 22% income tax bracket, and do the conversion in March, then you hit a scratch-off later in the year or Aunt Tilly leaves you a cool million? Right, boo-hoo, who's complaining? But you will pay more taxes on that conversion than you'd planned. That said, some people will take advantage of any huge market drop to do a chunk of their planned conversion. This is optimal because pulling those deflated shares out when the market has dropped, and watching them re-inflate tax free when the market recovers, is pretty fun.

The moral of the story here is don't let your pretax retirement funds blow up over the years to where you'll be in the very high income tax brackets during those latter years when you're forced to take required minimum distributions. As well, if you load up your Roth, you'll be able to use that money, rather than taxable distributions, to live on. If you do that prior to taking Social Security, you then have more space to convert in your taxable income brackets. A benefit here is that when you do get to taking Social

Security, less of it will be taxable, as you can live off that additional tax-free Roth money. It's also a tax-free inheritance to anyone you leave it behind for. One last benefit is that it allows you to get ahead of any future tax hikes, such as when the Tax Cuts and Jobs Act is slated to expire at the end of 2025.

Be wary of things like long-term care costs late in life, however. Those are essentially tax-free if they're high enough to allow you to itemize your deductions. So, if you're planning to spend $150,000 in your final years on LTC, don't convert that. Leave it sitting in your IRA. Don't pay taxes on something that won't be taxed! Same idea if you have any other years ahead when you'll be able to itemize your deductions for things like huge medical expenses (not unusual late in life either). If you don't intend to use the IRA money, don't convert it and pay the taxes on it, unless you're doing that as a favor to any heirs you're leaving it to. If you're leaving it to charity, they don't get taxed, so don't convert it.

Young people who intend to follow the FIRE lifestyle and retire early will usually put all their money into traditional accounts like 401k/403b/457 while working, and use those early-retired FIRE years when they have low or no income to do conversions at 0% to 12% and let it grow tax free. But you can't just yank the money out! Be careful or you'll get nailed with penalties and maybe even taxes. We'll talk about that more in a moment.

Backdoor Roth Conversions If you make above a certain amount of earned income, you can't make an annual Roth IRA contribution. But you can use this backdoor strategy to accomplish it. You would put the money into a traditional IRA as an after-tax deposit (meaning, it's not pretax like normal IRA contributions to be taxed later). Then, before there can be any gains, you immediately move the money to a Roth. This is complicated and fraught with ways to screw it up, so we don't recommend it.

It's cleaner and works better if you have no IRA money currently, otherwise you subject yourself to a nightmare called the "pro rata" rule. As we don't recommend it, we won't say more.

In-Plan Roth Conversions (Mega-Backdoor) Some retirement plan sponsors, like Fidelity, will automatically handle something like the backdoor technique above for you, within your 401k plan. After you've contributed the maximum to your 401k, they then move any excess contributions to a Roth 401k for you. This is a much cleaner solution, and they're doing all the dirty work, so we approve this one. It can only be done up to the max $66k total annual employee plus employer contribution ($73.5 if over 50), but it starts the tax-free growth and five-year conversion clock right away, and lowers RMDs later in life.

Roth Five-Year Clocks There are multiple five-year clocks on Roth accounts. These determine when you're eligible to withdraw money without being penalized and/or taxed. Please refer back to the start of this section to distinguish **conversions** versus **contributions**. It's important for this topic. An important ground rule to establish right off the bat is that you can withdraw your Roth **contributions** (not the gain on them!) at any time for any reason at any age. For **conversions**, not so much. There is one bright spot—the clock starts ticking on the first day of the year you open the account or do the conversion. So, if you do it late in the year, the clock starts on the first of the year. If you made the contribution for the prior year when you do your taxes in April, the clock begins on the first day of the prior year. Even if you close the account, the clock keeps ticking!

Let's talk more about the **contributions**. We said you could take your basis (contributed money) any time you want, no strings attached. The ability to take the earnings/growth for contributions depends on how long it's been since you opened any Roth IRA, and your own age. You must have had a Roth account for at least five years. It doesn't have to be this particular one, but one must have been in place for that period of time. Secondly, you must be at least 59 1/2 years old. Otherwise, it's taxes and 10% penalties on the earnings you withdraw. There are exceptions for buying your first home, education expenses, death/disablement, birth/adoption of a child, and medical expenses. You still pay the taxes in those cases if you haven't had a Roth open for at least five years, but you avoid the penalty.

Now let's talk about the five-year rule for **conversions**. In this case, each individual Roth conversion has its own five-year rule, and you can't touch any of it until that clock has expired, or you pay the penalty, unless you're older than age 59 1/2.

The last Roth five-year clock is on **inherited** Roth IRAs. You can withdraw money at any time, but if the Roth wasn't open for at least five years when the person died, you'll pay taxes. You can leave it sit until the five-year mark hits, or even disclaim the inheritance if you don't want it. As with inherited traditional IRAs, spouses and others have different rules as far as how much time they have until the account has to be emptied.

It's important to note that the IRS doesn't track your contribution/conversion "lots" specifically in regard to all this. All your Roth IRAs look like one big Roth IRA to them, and they just keep track of the total amount in the overall contributions, conversions, and earnings buckets. Each time you take money from any Roth IRA, the IRS reduces the balance in those buckets accordingly. So, your withdrawals come from contributions, until that's exhausted. Then from conversions, then from earnings. Even if you contributed $100k and due to poor market performance that money has shrunk to $80k, it's still $100k to the IRS for this computation. There's no need to do complex tracking on your end! The recommendation is to get your first Roth IRA open as soon as possible, so the five-year clock that relies on account age begins ticking. You could do that with a Roth contribution if you're eligible, or if not do a small $100 Roth conversion to get the account open.

Capital Gains Taxes

We talked about how your income is taxed. We also said in the last chapter that your Roth accounts aren't taxed as long as you obey the withdrawal rules, and your traditional/pretax accounts (regular IRAs, 401k/403b/457) plans are taxed just like income when you withdraw from them in retirement. Bonds, checking, savings pay interest, which is taxed along with income. The next most common type of tax is capital gains tax. Think of this as a tax on assets you own that have grown in value, for example, a vacation home, classic/antique car, or....stocks! Let's focus on that latter example.

Ok, we're talking brokerage accounts here, since we covered the other primary types of accounts. Let's say you buy 100 shares of VTI at $200 a share. You paid $20,000 for that *lot* of 100 shares (remember that term). Two years later, the price per share has grown to $225. That means each of the 100 shares you own is worth $25 more than you paid for it. It also means you have a $2,500 *unrealized* gain in your investment in VTI. Your statement should show that. You don't get taxed on unrealized gain, so all is cool. It looks nice on your portfolio value in your statement, though!

If you decide to sell the shares, that's when you *realize* that formerly *unrealized* gain, and it becomes taxable. Since you owned the shares longer than a year, they're subject to long-term capital gains tax (LTCG). This type of tax currently has only three brackets—0%, 15%, and 20%. Which bracket you're in depends on your taxable income (see our earlier exercise). The LTCG brackets aren't progressive. In 2023, if you're single and your taxable income is $44,625 or less, your LTCG rate is 0%, sweet! But if you make one dollar more of taxable income, it goes to 15% and the whole LTCG is taxed at that rate. It's not a progression through brackets like income tax. That's why it's so important to be aware of and manage these brackets for tax decisions. It's why we use a high-powered tool to wrangles those cats for our clients.

That said, 15% isn't a bad tax rate at all. We all wish we could forever be in the 15% income tax bracket, because income tax brackets can go as high as 37%. Once you're in the 15% LTCG bracket, you're pretty much good to go. The next and final bracket, 20%, doesn't kick in until up around $500k for most people. But what if you sold those shares of VTI prior to having owned them for more than a year? What if you sold them after holding them exactly a year or less? In that case, your gain falls into the short-term capital gains area, which is taxed just like regular income. It's the same drill for a non-primary residence, like a vacation home, investment property, and so on. Your primary home is safe from LTCG for up to $250k per person (or $500k married/joint) gain over what you paid and invested in improvements, per married couple.

Harvesting

Tax Gain Harvesting What we just covered means that in your prime working years, you'll probably be in the 15% bracket. But if you take a sabbatical (like we mentioned with the hack in the college chapter), mini-retirement, not working because of health issues, early retired/FIRE, or regular retired, you may well sit in that 0% LTCG bracket. That's when you want to do ***tax gain harvesting***, which is choosing that opportune year to cash out some of those unrealized gains on the cheap (like, zero cheap!).

Tax Loss Harvesting What if you had a loss on those VTI shares? Suppose they drop to $175, meaning you're down $25 on each of your 100 shares, $2,500 total. If you sell after you've held them for more than a year, you can write that realized loss off on your taxes. Not a terrible deal! If it exceeds the $3,000 per year limit, you can save the rest and write that off next year. That's called tax loss harvesting. It helps during your prime earning years and you have a big tax bill.

For example, you may have bought some high-expense clunker investments prior to reading this book. Selling them at a loss solves two problems—you get a tax break, and you get to exit the position you regret and buy something better. If you're intending to do this, and a huge stock market drops (as is happening as I write this!), that's a great time to sell and get that bigger tax break. It can cancel out any realized gains you have during the same year.

Be careful though, you can't just sell those VTI shares at a loss in your brokerage and then turn around and buy more. That's called a ***wash sale***, and it's prohibited. You can buy anything else except something that's "substantially" the same within thirty days of selling. So, you could buy a S&P 500 index fund, then sell it after thirty days and buy VTI again. Don't mess with the IRS. These transactions are tracked and reported.

Dividends

What about dividends? How are they taxed? Well, there are two kinds of dividends—qualified and non-qualified (aka, "ordinary"). Most mutual fund/ETF stocks and funds issue qualified dividends. Non-qualified/ordinary dividends are ones that result from insurance company premium returns, dividends that credit unions return to their members, or from tax-exempt organizations, real-estate investment trusts, co-ops, or employee stock ownership plans. If you're doing plain-Jane investing as we recommend, your dividends in your brokerage account will be qualified dividends. There's one more circumstance where they might be considered non-qualified, which is complicated and related to how long you've held the shares, i.e. you bought and sold them within a short period, which is the behavior we don't recommend. Qualified dividends otherwise are taxed at those LTCG brackets.

If your 100 VTI shares pay out $4 per share total this year, you'd have made $400 in qualified dividend income. Don't confuse this with unrealized gains, which, as we said, is an increase in the value of the shares. When you get dividends, you got paid, even if you choose to reinvest those dividends in new shares automatically (a good practice in the wealth accumulation stage of your life). Your brokerage will note this, and include the info in your 1099-DIV form, to be factored in when you do your tax return.

Because of the benefits of the LTCG tax rates, some retirees will live off their dividends and never sell the shares. They leave them behind to their heirs, who then get a step-up on the basis (share value) when they take ownership, meaning the unrealized gains that have piled up over all those years are erased. Same thing with the value of a primary home you leave them!

Asset Location

As we saw above, LTCG tax rates are more favorable than income tax rates, at least when you have a lot of earned income. Because of that, it's a strategic move to keep your bond holdings in your retirement accounts and mostly stock in your brokerage account. That kind of strategic placement of your money is called **asset location** planning. It's great if you're a plan-it-to-the-penny type of person, or have a great deal of money/income from the bond holdings. But for most people, it doesn't make a huge difference and may not be worth the extra hassle of managing. Don't forget, if your bonds are in bond funds, not individual bonds, those are technically equity/stock funds. Only the dividends are taxed as regular income. Any shares in those bond funds sold later at a gain will be taxed per LTCG, just like stock funds, if you've held them longer than a year.

In brokerage accounts, it's more optimal to hold index funds/ETFs. They don't trade very often, so they have less 'churn' that leads to share sales and realized gains within the funds. Funds can and often do pay out their capital gains at the end of the year, though, for the individual shares held within the funds themselves. ETFs are more tax-efficient than regular mutual funds, because of the way they trade. It's another reason they're uber-popular.

In tax-deferred accounts, such as retirement accounts you haven't been taxed on yet but will when you withdraw, it's best to hold taxable bonds, real estate investment trust (REIT) funds, active funds with high turnover and yearly capital gain distributions.

As we mentioned earlier, another ingredient in this recipe is municipal bonds. Their interest/dividend payments aren't taxed at the federal level, and in some states aren't taxed at the state level, as long as the municipalities held are in your state.

Here's an asset location example for a retiree that's in the 24% tax bracket. Suppose they have a 60/40 portfolio. The 60% stocks are all in the brokerage, and the 40% bonds are in their traditional pretax IRA. They need to withdraw $20k this year. If they take it all from the IRA, they'll pay $20k x 24%, or $4,800, roughly (remember that whole effective tax rate thing). If they take it from the brokerage (assuming its dividends paid out and/or selling shares owned over a year) it's $20k x 15% (LTCG rate), or $3,000. You'd rather pay $3,000 than $4,800, right? If you're more wealthy, and in the 35% income tax bracket, the difference is more drastic. We'll talk about how to plan and execute retirement distributions in a later chapter.

Tax Avoidance vs Tax Evasion

Always remember the difference in these two terms. Tax avoidance is perfectly legal. Never pay more than you owe, and work to achieve that goal. Tax evasion is taking illegal, evasive moves to get out of paying taxes you owe. Don't do that. The room and food are free in prison, but it's not an optimal retirement location.

Tax Planning

Most certified public accountants (CPAs) are tax ***preparers***. Their job, and what they get measured by, is to save you the most money possible on taxes ***this year***. They typically are not forward looking tax planners or strategists. As you've seen above, there are plenty of examples where intentionally paying more taxes now, in terms of harvesting or Roth conversions, can reap huge rewards throughout the rest of your life. If you use a CPA to do your taxes, we recommend finding one that does long-term tax planning. Or, enlist a financial advisor/planner that includes this in your overall holistic financial roadmap, since most CPAs don't look at more than taxes. This puzzle has lots of moving parts, such as your investments, plans for the future, etc. They should all work in harmony.

For my clients and planning, I use an excellent tool called Pralana Retirement Calculator (pralanaretirementcalculator.com) that does all this long-term planning. You can buy and use it as well! It's amazing, but be forewarned, it's a very high fidelity tool that requires a basic knowledge of all the topics covered in this book. Mistakes can be expensive. We'll talk about it more in the retirement planning chapter.

You could also get the tax calculator at dinkytown.net toward the end of the year and start gaming some of this out yourself at the end of the year, as far as how much Roth to convert or gains to harvest.

Final Word on Investing/Taxes

We've covered a lot of hacks regarding taxes, laddering, asset location tricks, and much more that you can use to optimize every penny. If you're right up against the wire in regard to your financial plans, you may need to utilize every one of them. But, if you're OK otherwise, it may not be worth the time and work to try to do each one of these, unless you're totally into it. If you have a huge portfolio, these optimizations can pay off big, but again if you aren't into it, in that case you can afford to enlist an expert or two to do some of the work for you. Remember, it's about low stress, happiness, and enjoying this one life!

> *"I will tell you the secret to getting rich on Wall Street. You try to be greedy when others are fearful. And you try to be fearful when others are greedy."*

CHAPTER THIRTEEN

Social Security/Medicare

BE A SAVVY OLDIE

"Social Security is not just another government spending program. It is a promise from generation to generation."

Hank Johnson

Social Security

Want to ace your Social Security (SS) hack? It's easy, as long as you know when you're going to die. Therein lies the rub. But, we don't, so the question of when to claim Social Security can be quite tricky. Let's learn all about it and then discuss tactics.

Here's the deal. During their working years, workers and employers split a payroll tax to fund the Social Security trust fund.

You might see it listed on your paystub as OASDI, which stands for Old-Age, Survivors, and Disability Insurance. A few employers that provide pensions don't take part in the SS system, so in that case, neither do you. We'll get to that later, but you should know if yours doesn't, it's important for retirement planning! You only pay Social Security taxes up to $160,200 of earned income (2023 number). After that, your paycheck gets fatter because OSASDI no longer comes out. Some question whether this is fair, because high-income people get a big break there, and still get to collect Social Security even if they're very wealthy retirees.

While you're working, you are essentially paying for those who are collecting, as will some young whippersnappers pay for you when you're retired. The trust fund acts as a buffer. Try not to get too worked up when some scream about the trust fund being in trouble. Even if it were depleted, it doesn't mean payments will stop, because there are still millions and millions of workers funding the system.

You have to qualify before you can get access to that money someday. Just making the payroll deductions doesn't do it. You must earn 40 work credits in order to qualify (but your eventual monetary benefits aren't based on those). If you're going to do FIRE or retire early, and want benefits someday, make sure not to retire before you've qualified!

Fortunately, it's easy to earn credits. If you make at least $1,640 in earnings in 2023, that's one credit. Earn $6,560 during the year and you have four credits. One tenth of the way there already! Therefore, most people qualify after working for a decade or more. Related programs like Social Security Disability Insurance (SSDI) can require as few as six credits. There's no work requirement for Supplemental Security Income (SSI) which is for people who have very limited income and financial assets, and are aged or disabled.

Okie dokie, so you're qualified. How much do you get? That's determined by a formula that factors in the highest 35 years of earnings on your record. So, if you've only worked 30 years, consider doing more time and fill in those zero years. The empty slots can really work against you. Or, at least, like many early retirees or FIRE people, have a nice small business or side hustle to bring in some income, earn credits if you give yourself a proper paycheck, and provide some tax breaks.

Because 35 years is a long time, your earnings up through the year you turn 60 are indexed for wage inflation, so those earlier, skimpy earning years (by comparison) are brought up to par by the algorithm. They take the highest 35 years after applying this formula. Before you turn 62 your future benefit will be increased based on changes in wage growth. After you turn 62, the increases are based on consumer goods price inflation (you get these whether you have filed yet or not). What does that mean? There's one year, the year you turn 61, that you get no inflation benefit to your future Social Security PIA. This is called the Social Security **donut hole**. It can stink if there's high inflation that year, but in the grand scheme of things, it's not such a big deal.

The average payment is around $1,600 per month per person, or just over $3k per couple. The most you can make as of this writing is $3,627/month per person. It's not a huge amount, so have a plan. Don't rely solely on Social Security for your retirement! You should create a login at ssa.gov if you don't already have one, and download your statement regularly. Do that now, and refer to it during this chapter!

If you held a job at an employer that doesn't participate in Social Security, but provides a pension, and you also worked at jobs where you did have SS taxes withheld, your benefit will be reduced by something called the Windfall Elimination Provision (WEP). That won't show up on your SS statement, so if you believe you're affected, use one of the calculators we mention to figure out the damage. If you get no benefit or a much lower benefit, filing for spousal benefits (see below) may be an option. On the reverse side of this, if your spouse wants to file spousal benefits and you're affected by WEP, their spousal benefit will be lowered (in this case it's called the Government Pension Offset (GPO)). If you're affected by WEP, that penalty dies with you—it doesn't affect survivor benefits.

Case Study: I've seen many, many examples where my clients received incorrect information from the folks in the Social Security office (in-person and on the phone). Those people are under-trained, overworked, and underpaid. It's a stressful job. Do not rely on the information you receive verbally from them.

When to Claim

The biggest debate is when to start your benefit. You can collect your own Social Security benefit as early as age 62, but the earlier you start your benefit, the lower that monthly payment will be (about a 5% per year less). Depending on your year of birth, you're assigned a Full Retirement Age (FRA). For anyone born in 1960 or after, their FRA is age 67. For people born before 1960, it's younger (age 66 and change for most people). That's when your monthly payment stops getting discounted 5% per year for claiming early, and you get your "full" benefit, also called your Primary Insurance Amount, or PIA. Remember those two acronyms, FRA and PIA! When you figure out the month you want to start benefits, file a few months in advance, as applications are slow to process. Just make sure to designate your future starting month on the application.

The fun doesn't stop there—if you wait longer than your FRA to claim, your monthly payment is jacked up even more with bonus money (around 8% per year). You can wait as long as up to age 70 for the bonus. After that, there's no sense in waiting, because your payment won't get bigger for waiting. Are you suspecting something? Yes, along with our friends in the insurance/annuity business, they're hoping they can tempt you into waiting to collect your benefit, and you die in the interim. Then you get nuttin,' honey. No money to leave behind, either.

You see tons of advice to wait at least until FRA to collect. But what if you've got health issues and longevity doesn't run in your family? That's certainly a factor in deciding to claim early. For example, suppose your benefit is $2,000 per month at age 62. If you wait until FRA at age 67, you've missed out on five years of payments, or $120,000. You could have enjoyed that money, retired instead of staying on the miserable hamster wheel, and maybe left it behind to your loved ones or charity. Many folks who don't need the money say, "I'll just invest it, I can beat that 5% penalty with index funds, since I'm getting inflation increases automatically." Be aware though, the total reduction in your monthly payment by claiming at 62 instead of FRA is 30%.

The break-even point from waiting until FRA usually occurs in your early to mid 80s. Some people say, "What am I going to do with the extra money at that age? I could have been having more fun in my go-go years of retirement!" My point is that, along with the theme of this book, it's not always a math decision. Sometimes it's a mental health or happiness decision. The actuaries at the Social Security department who figure all this out are actually trying to make sure that you end up with the same amount overall, no matter when you claim, so it's not such a big deal to claim earlier, as long as the math works (see below). In a nutshell, collect earlier if you're pretty certain you won't have longevity (and have a backup plan in case you live longer than expected!), or the quality of life now outweighs possible mathematical gain later. On the flip side, it's no small thing that this is a lifetime income stream that's adjusted for inflation. That's pretty hard to come by! So, if you don't need it, maybe hold back and let 'er grow.

It's an important decision, and you should do your own math using your latest SS statement. You should have a solid financial/retirement plan (as we'll discuss in the next chapter) that outlines whether you'll risk running out of money by claiming too early, among other factors. Once you make this decision to start Social Security, it's difficult to undo! You can change your mind within the first year and reverse it, but you have to pay back every penny. Do you still have it in the bank, or is it at the racetrack or Bally's? Don't laugh. I used to be a professional blackjack dealer at Sands Casino—I've seen it happen! Always factor in the decision that Social Security is inflation-adjusted income for the rest of your life, which is a pretty big deal. We'll talk about a few other ways to back this decision off later in this chapter.

We will not go into the nuances of disability. (Social Security is another topic that can be a book of its own, and there are some good ones out there). If you qualify for SSDI, that payment is your PIA, even if you qualify prior to your FRA (or even before age 62).

Working and Receiving Social Security

If you claim before you reach FRA, and you intend to continue working (even part time), be careful how much income you earn. This "earned income test" problem goes away after you hit your FRA (regardless of when you started benefits). But until then, if you earn more than $21,240 during the year from work (earned income), they will lower your benefit by $1 per month for every $2 you made over that limit. Communicate with Social Security and let them know. If they figure it out after you've filed your tax return the following year, they'll withhold checks until you make up that deduction. The limit turns into $56,520 during the year you reach FRA, and they only dock $1 for every $3 over the limit. Those are 2023 numbers and they will change. But, there's a silver lining—the lost money isn't gone forever. You get it back as increased monthly payments after you hit your FRA.

And don't worry, if you're working part-time, those lower earnings can't hurt your Social Security benefit, only help them. It's based on the highest 35 years of earnings.

The above earnings test could constitute a hack to undo taking Social Security early. Go back to work and earn gobs of money to make your payments disappear, and get them back later as those increased monthly payments when you really, really retire. The income you are receiving also counts as far as the highest 35 years on your record, so you could actually increase your benefit during this time! Win-win. You can erase any zero years, or bump up any of the lowest earning years. The second hack is that you can pause your benefit when you reach FRA, and those 8%/year bonus credits are applied all the way to age 70, plus COLA increases.

Social Security and Taxes

Will your Social Security income itself be taxed? Most likely, yes, but only some of it, and never all of it. At the federal income tax level, there's a formula for determining this. You'd take that MAGI number we talked about in the last chapter, add any non-taxable interest payments (such as municipal bond interest), and half your annual Social Security benefit. If that's above $25k (single) or

$32k (married/joint) you'll get taxed on half your Social Security income for the year. The tax rate is determined via the methods we discussed in the previous chapter, but again, only half the amount you earned is taxed at that point.

The scale continues as your income grows. Note, this factors in not just earned income, but also taxable retirement distributions. The most they'll tax out of your annual Social Security income is 85% of it. That 85% threshold hits when you cross over $34k single/$44k married/joint. Be clear, that doesn't mean you're paying an 85% tax rate! It's taxed through the progressive tax tables, and your effective tax is likely low in retirement. And unlike the earnings test we discussed earlier, this tax on a portion of your SS income happens until you die.

This SS taxing can be a problem, though, if you've worked part of the year, earned big bucks, and want to retire in the same year and start collecting. In that case, it may be better to wait until the new year to file. If you've reached your FRA, here's another hack! You can wait until the first week in January, and file retroactively. That means you can say you want to start your filing date up to six months into the past, reaching back into that prior year when you made all that money at the job, but the big lump sum check they send you is taxed in the new/current year, when your tax rates are likely much lower. Another way to defeat this problem, especially if you haven't reached FRA yet, is to ask for the earnings test to be applied monthly going forward from your filing date. That takes the partial-year big earnings prior to when you retired off the board. You can only do that once, in the year you first file for benefits.

The tax issue is another reason to take advantage of those years prior to claiming Social Security. You can mitigate some of this by taking larger retirement distributions in those years, or living off already taxed money like brokerage or Roth, keeping your tax rates ultra low, and doing larger Roth conversions on the cheap.

Spousal Benefits

Here's another widely misunderstood feature of Social Security, particularly for divorced people. Let's get this straight—if you're divorced for at least two years, and you were married over ten years, and currently single (even if you remarried to someone else in the interim) you can claim spousal benefits without the knowledge or permission of your ex. It doesn't affect their benefits in the least, and they aren't notified. Got that? It's a no-drama zone.

Spousal benefits come in handy when one spouse has a much lower SS benefit than the other. If you wait until your FRA, you can get up to 50% of your spouse (or ex) full benefit (PIA). If you're still married to the person, they must have already started collecting. If you're divorced, they must only be eligible to have started, but don't need to have actually started. That rule was created to stop malicious exes from holding off just to screw over their former spouse. If you take spousal benefits earlier than your FRA, the benefit, just like your regular benefit, will be reduced.

A little known fact is that when you claim spousal benefits, you're really claiming your own benefit. It's just topped up with the spousal part. So, there's no claiming spousal now, and "switching" to your own later (unless you were born before 1954). It's a done deal unless your spouse or ex dies, then we get into survivor benefit, which you *can* switch to after starting your own or spousal benefit.

Case Study: I had a client who was married to their ex spouse for just shy of ten years. What a shame! I dug and fought for her, but there's no appeal process. It's a hard and fast rule.

Survivor Benefits

You can collect survivor benefits as early as age 60, or even 50 if you're disabled. Again, if you're less than FRA, the benefit will be discounted, and it depends on your former spouse's age and benefit (if collecting) upon their death. If they were already collecting, you just assume that benefit. However, if they had collected early, as a survivor, your survivor benefit is adjusted higher so you aren't hurt as much by that decision. If they weren't collecting, it would be their full benefit even if they weren't at their FRA yet. If they were older than FRA and in the 8% bonus period, your survivor benefit is what theirs would have been on the date they deceased.

Unlike spousal benefits, you can claim the survivor benefit even if yours is lower, and just let yours grow! Most people aren't aware of that hack. You qualify for survivor benefits even if you were divorced, and even if you remarried after age 60. This benefit allows things like starting the survivor benefit at age 60, two years earlier than normal eligibility, collecting that money, and letting your own benefit grow until FRA or up to age 70.

Social Security Disability (SSDI)

You can file for disability right until your full retirement age and collect your FRA PIA early. After your FRA, that's what you'd get anyway, so no sense going through the hassle. You can also have earned income of $1,470 a month ($2,460 if you are blind) in 2023 while on SSDI. Short- and long-term disability, vacation/sick days, and other forms of non-earned income don't count toward that.

How to Optimize Your Benefits

I like to use a free tool at opensocialsecurity.com. Click the little checkbox at the top to open up all the inputs. Game out some scenarios for yourself and your spouse/partner if you have one. The author of that site, Mike Piper, has his great SS book for sale there. There's a paid tool as well at maximizemysocialsecurity.com.

Social Security Myths

There's so much misinformation out there! Here are some myths.
- The fund is going broke - not true, but changes need to be made

- Retirement age is 65 - not true, can collect any time starting at 62

- Yearly cost-of-living adjustment is guaranteed - it's not, but there usually is one

- Congress doesn't pay in, they get it free - no longer true

- Government raids the account for other stuff - not true, but they borrow from it! Former President Reagan borrowed massive amounts and never paid it back, a big factor in the current trust fund deficit (see: The Great Social Security Heist of 1983).

- Undocumented workers deplete the account - actually they contribute tens of billions and never get to use it! Thank them.

- It's like a savings account at 8% interest if you want - not true - you don't get the 'principal' and most years it's 5%

- You don't pay taxes on it - not true - you may have to pay federal and state taxes

- Your ex's benefits will come out of yours if they file spousal benefits - not true

- You lose the money deducted because you exceeded the earnings limit - not true

- If you had a non-FICA pension you can't collect - not true, but use the calculators I mentioned to figure the WEP damage

Medicare

Medicare is a US government federal health insurance program that subsidizes health care. It covers people 65 or older, as well as young people who meet specific eligibility criteria. The first and most fundamental thing to understand about Medicare is that it's broken out in 'parts':

- Part A covers hospitalization (this part is free if you paid in for ten years while working). The first $1,600 of services are on you, and the first 60 days of hospital days are covered. If you need to stay between 61 and 90 days, the tab is $400/day. After that, you have a lifetime reserve of 60 days at $800/day. You're on the hook for anything additional.

- Part B covers doctor visits, specialists, outpatient visits/surgery, ambulances, wellness, mammograms, cardio screening, telehealth, and more. Most people pay a low $164 monthly premium. The first $226 of services are on you and after your deductible, you pay 20%.

- Part C is called Medicare Advantage (we'll discuss later)

- Part D covers drugs/prescriptions (finally, one that's easy to remember, D for Drugs!). You pay a monthly premium usually between $12-$76/month

When to Sign Up

As we saw earlier in this chapter, you have lots of leeway in regard to signing up for Social Security. Not so with Medicare! Don't screw this up, it could be expensive. If you're collecting Social Security, you get signed up automatically for parts A & B. Otherwise, you can register within three months of your 65th birthday, your birthday month, and three months after. That seven months comprise your **initial enrollment period**. I recommend you use it to enroll, even if you're covered by an employer health plan. You can sign up for just Part A, which is free. If you work for a small employer (fewer than 20 employees), you might have to sign up, anyway.

Otherwise, remember to sign up within eight months of leaving that employer and their health plan. This is called the **special enrollment period**, and it's what you don't want to screw up. If you miss your special enrollment, you must wait for **general enrollment** (between January 31 and March 31) and the coverage will be more expensive. There are penalties and your coverage doesn't start until July 1. Don't tempt fate.

The normal **annual open enrollment** period is mid-October through early December. You can change your plan at that time if you're already enrolled. The current Part B premium in 2023 is about $164/month. Part D averages about $30/month. Average annual costs for Medicare (including out-of-pocket) are between $4,200-$6,000 per person.

Choosing the right Medicare plan can be very confusing, and mistakes are expensive. There are specialists who can guide you, and most are free or very inexpensive. They usually get paid commission, so it's important to find one that will put your best interests first, not sign you up for the plan that pays them the most. You can get help at shiphelp.org.

Part A and Part B are called "traditional" or "original" Medicare. Then you can tack on the Part D coverage for prescriptions. There are lots of Part D choices! The right one for you depends on exactly what medicines you take, so look at the options carefully. Your spouse might do better on a different one than you. There's a pretty good tool for finding/picking choices at medicare.gov/find-a-plan/questions/home.aspx.

IRMAA

IRMAA isn't that crotchety old aunt of yours. It stands for Income Related Monthly Adjustment Amount. If your Modified Adjusted Gross Income during retirement is more than $97k (individual) or $194k (married/joint) you find yourself in IRMAA-land. That means your Medicare premiums will be adjusted upwards as your income grows beyond that point. The brackets are cliffs—one dollar over, and you (and your spouse, if married) make the monthly payment amount for that bracket. This is another reason it's important to be careful with things like Roth conversions, as discussed in the last chapter.

When you enroll, your previous two years of income are used to determine your rate. Of course, if you just retired, you don't have that income anymore, so why should you be forced to pay more? You shouldn't, and you won't, if you file an SSA-44 to explain the situation. They'll adjust if you just left your job and no longer have that work income. They won't adjust if it's because of a Roth conversion or home sale, so be careful with those!

Medigap Coverage

Parts A, B, and D don't cover things like vision, dental, hearing aids, and podiatry (foot care). You can buy what's called Medigap coverage to fill in those "gaps." Medigap sub-plans are assigned letters A through G, with different price levels and benefits. When you sign up for the first time, there is no medical exam required. They can't deny you for any preexisting conditions. Put a pin on that thought, it will be important shortly. They deduct your Part B premium from your Social Security check, if you're collecting. You can pay the Part D premium or any Medigap premium directly out-of-pocket or through your SS payment.

Medicare Advantage

Notice I have said little about Part C—Medicare Advantage. It's a whole other thing, that's why! This is actually private insurance that may take over your Medicare as long as they can provide substantially equal or better coverage. It has to cover everything traditional Medicare does. You'll see it offered by familiar names like Cigna and United Healthcare. It's an enormous industry all to its own, which is why you get bombarded with those horrible, sometimes misleading commercials.

Advantage plans tend to cover all the extras that are missing from traditional Medicare, but be careful, because they might be pretty limited in coverage. They're structured like either HMOs or PPOs, so be careful if they restrict you to a particular group of physicians or hospitals. Ask if your travel plans will be covered! Advantage plans are a better choice for relatively healthy people, but can be more expensive than traditional plus Medigap for people with chronic health conditions. The premiums might be lower with Advantage plans, but your total out-of-pocket cost for lots of care might be a lot more.

If you join a Medicare Advantage plan, you'll get your Medicare benefits from the private insurance company instead of from government's "original Medicare." You still pay Medicare Part B premiums, and that gets transferred to your Advantage insurance company to help pay for your benefits.

If you sign up for Advantage/Part C and regret it, you can go back to traditional/Medigap within a year (trial period). But after that, you're exposed to having to take a physical and maybe getting denied for preexisting conditions. There are a few states that don't allow this discrimination and allow you to switch back without the underwriting/physical. Be very careful with this choice, and as with any trial, mark that ending date on your calendar.

Medicare and Long-Term Care

Medicare doesn't cover LTC expenses! It will pay for nursing home and rehab costs for 21 days. After that, it goes to $200/day. However, if you run out of assets, Medicaid will cover costs. Veterans receive care from the Veteran's Administration.

Medicare Savings Accounts

These are similar to Advantage plans—they're also offered by private insurance companies. They offer similar add-ons like dental and vision, but they're high-deductible plans, which can be dangerous if you have a lot of health problems. They include an HSA-like bank account, which the plan puts money into for you. You're required to have Part A and Part B coverage to participate, and can enroll when you first sign up during open enrollment or the special enrollment period. They're not available everywhere.

Limited Income Help

If you have limited resources, there's help. Check into some of the below programs.

- Medicare Savings Programs

- State Pharma Assistance Programs

- Qualified Medicare Beneficiary Program (QMB)

- Qualifying Individual Program (QI)

- Qualified Disabled and Working Individuals (QDWI)

- State Health Insurance Assistance Program (SHIP) - free advice/counseling

Chapter Fourteen

(Early?) Retirement Planning

FIRE or Trad, Let's Do This!

"And in the end it's not the years in your life that count. It's the life in your years."

Abraham Lincoln

Now we get to my love language, finally! I'm talking about planning your freedom, plotting your escape from the doldrums and hamster wheel. However, heed my warning. If you're miserable, think things through. Is it really the job, or other factors? Money? We fixed that already, hopefully, in these pages. If it's something else, freedom from the job and money stress may not solve it. Be honest with yourself. That's what the beginning of this chapter is all about. Have a long, thorough heart-to-heart with yourself about why you might be unhappy and what would make you happy. That's what we want to accomplish, after all.

Accumulation vs Enjoyment Phases

When you're young and in your working years, you're in the retirement asset accumulation phase. At least, we hope so! Some folks get caught up in the moment, wanting everything possible now, and do great harm to their future selves.

"I'll start contributing next year."
"I'll start contributing with my next raise."
"I'll start contributing after I pay the car off."

Don't be that person. It's foolish, especially if you're missing out on the free money you get from employer matching. It doesn't work, because of the tremendous impact that compounding has on those earliest contributions. You can't start late and hope to succeed. If you're justifying this behavior because you love your career and think you'll never mind working, I have news for you. You change as you get older. Your health changes. The employer or boss you love now can change with mergers and acquisitions. You may have kids and grandkids you're going to want to spend more time with and love more than work (gasp!).

The above is also the reason you should never borrow from your retirement accounts. Sure, it sounds like a swell deal. But you're only looking at the interest rate. The real, hidden damage is done by all the loss of those reinvested dividends and that growth and compounding while the money is out of the account. It's a very expensive way to borrow money, and just foolish unless you're about to lose your house and have already tried everything else in this book. After all I've taught you, it's hard to believe there isn't another way to come up with the money.

When you retire, you transition into the enjoyment phase. That means enjoyment of all the assets you've built up in the accumulation phase! It can actually be very difficult to transition from one to the other. We spend our whole lives (hopefully) treating that retirement savings as precious, hands-off, do not touch. It's a hard mentality to change, and why it's so important to have a detailed, high fidelity plan (discussed below) to give yourself permission and do so knowing there's very little risk.

Roth vs Traditional Retirement Accounts

When in accumulation phase and contributing to workplace retirement plans, the question often comes up, "Should I do the Roth or the traditional?" Ask yourself, "Do I want to pay the taxes now, or in retirement?" If you're early in your career, and perhaps in a 10%-15% marginal tax bracket, I'd pay that low rate (in general) and contribute to the Roth. As your income grows and you start bumping up into that 22% and higher range, I'd be looking at traditional contributions. The same logic applies when you file your taxes, if you find yourself eligible to contribute to either type of IRA. The same logic applies when deciding whether to do Roth conversions—is this a good time tax-rate-wise versus later in life when we're forced to take the money as required minimum distributions (RMDs)? Avoid creating a tax bomb for yourself in your later years.

Remember, when you contribute to a traditional workplace plan or traditional IRA, that amount is removed from your taxable income for the current year. You get a tax break now on that amount, and you pay the taxes on it later, if/when you take it from the account in retirement. That's what those RMDs are all about! As you get older, the government wants that tax money you've been owing them. They require you to start taking distributions from your untaxed money, so they can tax it. If you're not already subject to RMDs, you'll have to start at age 73 if you were born in 1959 or earlier, and age 75 if you were born in 1960 or after. Essentially, they divide your remaining years of life expectancy by your untaxed balance to calculate the annual RMD amount. With Roth accounts, there's no tax break today. You've already paid the taxes on that money, but the growth is tax free forever (a pretty big deal) and you can withdraw it without cost in retirement.

As discussed, some workplace plans have a cool feature called in-plan Roth conversions, where after you max out your contributions to traditional 401k/403b/457 type plans, they'll do automatic mega-backdoor conversions over to a Roth 401k. We talked about conversions back in the chapter on advanced investing and taxes.

Order of Contributions

The best *general* order of operations as far as where to put your money is below:

1. Have a solid 3-6 months of expenses in an emergency fund

2. Contribute to employer workplace plans (retirement and HSA) up to the match

3. Pay off your non-mortgage debt

4. Max out HSA and retirement contributions

5. Make any available annual IRA contributions at tax time

6. If you're saving money for your kids' education, do it here

7. Pay off your mortgage early (unless you have a crazy low rate)

8. Use extra money to pay taxes on strategic Roth conversions

9. Build up your brokerage accounts

FIRE (Financial Independence Retire Early)

I've mentioned the FIRE movement a few times. It stands for Financial Independence Retire Early. It's borne of the disruptive movement by young people, who ask the primary question, "Why should I wait until I'm old to stop working and enjoy life?" They've seen their grandparents, maybe parents, work on that hamster wheel long after they stopped enjoying it. They've seen many friends and relatives perhaps finally almost get to that cherished date, after working all their lives, and have it all taken away by a global pandemic—bucket lists unlived. FIRE advocates typically shoot for their 40s or 50s to become financially independent or retire early.

The FIRE movement has grown considerably. In fact, since most advocates really seek the financial independence part more than actual early retirement, it's been shorted in many cases to just FI. Many of them continue working after they've reached financial independence, but it sure feels different going into a job and knowing you don't have to be there!

There are a ton of FIRE bloggers—some very good, some not so much. Most people doing FIRE have a side hustle or small business, which we've advocated for in this book. They have an income small enough to keep them in the very lowest tax brackets, but enough to pay their expenses in a pseudo early retirement lifestyle, most times while traveling the country in an RV or living in exotic locations like Thailand or Costa Rica. Yes, even while homeschooling young kids! In fact, there's a sweet foreign income tax exclusion that they take advantage of while doing this.

Be careful though. Another way FIRE influencers make money on their blogs and social media is to push credit cards, which they get paid for by the credit card companies. As I said in Chapter 3, credit card hacking for points/miles is fine, if it's something you enjoy. But, it's work, and it can be dangerous. I don't recommend it, for reasons stated in the very first chapter of this book. Keep your financial life simple for the win.

How do FIRE people do it? They do exactly what I'm saying to do, which is disavow debt, be a smart consumer, pay less for everything, and save and invest wisely. They use their own rule of thumb called the FIRE number, which is associated with the 4% rule we talked about in the investing chapters. The FIRE number is 25 times your annual expenses. It's a very rough, high-level rule of thumb, which is a terrible thing to base a huge decision like retirement on! We'll see below that your expenses in different periods of your life will vary. We know that the 4% rule is based on a thirty-year retirement, which is significantly shorter than a typical early retiree would experience.

This is incredibly risky on many levels. You're cutting your accumulation phase very short, and losing that compounding effect we discussed above. You're extending your enjoyment phase quite a bit. A lot can happen, a lot can go wrong. Can you make it work? Sure, but you better have a precise plan with plenty of backups in place. Don't make this huge decision without careful planning. If things don't work out, it's going to be tough going back to work (not to mention getting someone to hire you) after experiencing that freedom. Don't base it on any rough rule of thumb! You'll need to deploy all the advice in this book from start to finish. In this chapter, I'll show you a far better way to map your FIRE journey out.

Plan Your Escape

You have to have a plan for your time in retirement. If you don't, you might quickly find yourself both lonely and unhappy, missing the social aspects, sense of purpose, and self-esteem that you may have gotten from the job. Too many people have retired, only to find companionship at Martini's Bar, and die of alcoholism. What were the things you enjoyed and dreamed about as a child? Get back in touch with that idealistic young person before life took over and hardened you.

Maybe you didn't end up being a pro baseball player, regrettably, but now's the time you can join the local recreational team, and increase your health and odds of a longer, happier retirement. Learn an instrument, playing music and/or singing can be *so* therapeutic and enhance longevity. If you get good, dare to go to your local open mic and entertain some folks. Don't forget to put out that tip jar! Volunteer, it's rewarding and brings back that sense of purpose in life. Write that great American novel. Be a legend, even if only in your own mind, because that's all that counts. Hopefully you've stopped worrying about impressing other people long ago.

Do you have a manifesto? Not like, a unibomber type one. A declaration of your wishes, hopes, and dreams. No, wait! A declaration of your **intent** for the rest of your life. Whether you're an early/FIRE or a traditional retiree, you've worked hard for this. This period should be everything you've ever dreamed it would be. Happiness. Before we get to the numbers and how to make them work:

Stop.

Close Your Eyes.

Dream About Your Perfect Retirement.

Let's go.

Awake now? Write that stuff down. Brainstorm with your significant other if you have one. So many have come to me and said, "I'll never get to retire. I'll work until I die." That's incredibly sad to hear, and for me, it's incredibly motivating. We get to work, and we get it done. Seeing their gloom turn to happiness and excitement is a reward I'll never get used to. That can be you!

Done dreaming? Let's get started and make those dreams into reality. So, what did you come up with? Travel? Pursuit of long-neglected hobbies? Moving somewhere warmer? A vacation/lake home? Being generous? The first step is to figure out what those things will cost. If you've been following the guidance in this book so far, you should have a pretty good idea of what your monthly expenses are right now. Write those down on a pad of paper, or in a spreadsheet.

Next to those current monthly expenses, make a new column. Call it "Go-Go." No, not the dancers (for you oldies like me) or the 80's rock group. This is for the early "go-go" years of retirement, when you're young and newly retired, excited to do all the things you've been dreaming about or missing out on by working. Your work/commute costs are gone, fun costs are up. Make another column and title it "Slow Go." These are the years, typically when you hit your early to mid 70s, when you slow down some. Not as much kayaking, hiking, mountain climbing, for most folks. Your expenses usually drop, and your pleasures may well come from spending time with the grandkids. Now, a last column titled "No Go." These are your more sedentary years, after you've hit 80 or so. We tend to eat less, take fewer vacations, but medical costs go up.

Look at that, you're planning your retirement. You're laying the foundation for those wondrous years ahead. Keep going! When you're done, you should have a monthly total/budget for each segment of your retirement years. Let's get that money together. We'll do some general projections first, then dial it in precisely.

Figure out what your monthly income will be in retirement. We just covered Social Security in the last chapter. That's a big part of your monthly income, in most cases. Do you have your statement handy, as we discussed? Put that monthly number down. Do you have any other forms of retirement income, such as a pension from an old employer? Check hard. There are billions of dollars out there from forgotten about pensions, retirement plans, stock options, and other employee benefits from old employers. Do that missing money exercise we talked about waaay at the beginning of this book. Add any of these to your Social Security.

Alrighty, how are we doing? Still short? We're not done yet!

The usual parts of retirement income (pension, Social Security) are pretty cut and dried after you make a few basic decisions. The part that stumps most people is their nest egg, meaning the total of money they have in their accounts. How much can you take without worrying about running out of money? That's the question. Most people I've seen do one of two things—they take too much, run out of money, and end up working at Walmart at 80 years old, or (most commonly) they're too afraid to use the money. The most common latter choice is disheartening. You worked for that money, enjoy it! This is why you saved it! They're just afraid they'll run out, in most cases. This is why old people have the unfair reputation of being "cheap." They're just afraid to spend and terrified of living on a fixed income and running out of money. Having a plan gives you permission to spend that well earned money on fun. How much? Let's answer that question.

The 4% Rule (of Thumb)

Because the answer to that question has been such a mystery, there was a study done called the Trinity Study. The purpose was to answer this question, and determine what a "safe withdrawal rate" would be, such that one could fully enjoy their money, but not risk overspending it and working at Walmart at 80 years old (unless, of course, that's what they desire and enjoy!). Here's what they found.

Start with the basic assumptions that you have your money invested reasonably, meaning somewhere between a 60/40 and 50/50 asset allocation (we talked about that in the investing chapters). If that's the case, you should be able to withdraw 4% in your first year, and adjust that for inflation each year, and then not run out of money for a typical thirty-year retirement. FIRE/early retirees take note! If you're early retiring at 40 years old, this will not work for you. We'll cover you later. Also, this is liquid assets only. Don't count your home value (unless you plan to sell it).

As an example, suppose you have a cool million stashed away. Four percent of that is $40,000 per year, or $3,333 a month in year one. At the end of year one, you check the inflation numbers and see the cost of living has gone up by 3%. You multiply your $40k by 1.03 and find your number for the new year is $41,200, or $3,433 per month. And so forth. Note that the 4% rule is flawed because, as you've already seen, your income needs vary in your retirement. 4% rule assumes you'll consistently take out 4% (plus inflation) until you die. In reality, it's still safe to tweak that and take more earlier, as long as you'll take less later. That's why you need a precise plan, a roadmap, instead of a high-level rule.

IMPORTANT: The 4% "rule" is really a rule of thumb, and I don't recommend retiring based on rules of thumb. It also assumes you will have normal investing fees. I've already shown you how to have almost zero fees. For now, it's a way to get a general idea of what kind of shape you're in. Apply the 4% math exercise to your nest egg, and add the monthly amount to your total. What's it telling you? Are you there yet? If so, you're good to go! If not, don't fret, we're just getting started. We'll show you how to fix it and probably be able to retire, anyway.

The 4% rule is very broad. Some people say it's too conservative! It's not factoring in things like asset location, for example. Suppose a bunch of your money is in brokerage (already taxed) and Roth (never taxed) accounts? That makes a big difference! Therefore, having a high-fidelity plan is the only way. It gives you the personalized, numerical, precision-guided proof and confidence to go forth and enjoy.

Fixes for Falling Short

If you're still not hitting that required monthly amount, at least for the go-go years, don't fret. Let's have a closer look. Can you cut back anywhere, at least until you get started and in the groove? Go back to those monthly expenses. Mark each essential expense, such as groceries, rent, utilities, healthcare, with an asterisk. Can you retire based on your essential expenses? That doesn't allow for much, if any, fun, but how much fun are you having at work? Hang on to that essential expenses total. We'll need that later when we pull out our power tools.

How much of those monthly expenses are debt payments? C'mon now! Job one is blowing those away. They're often the only thing holding people back from retirement. What's better, driving a 'status' car to a job you can't stand, or driving yourself to the beach every day in a used car with enough character to earn a name like Lady Agnes? If debt is the only thing holding you back, go to war on it. Re-read the early chapters of this book and devise a plan.

Are you willing to do something fun part-time, or enlist one of the side hustles in Chapter 3 to fire up a simple small business and get all the tax advantages? You have to do something with your time, after all. You may have been in a stressful teaching job, but like gardening. Go work at Lowe's garden center a few days a week, for just a few hours! Tell them you won't be around in the summer, you'll be at the beach. Or whatever. You're the boss now. Hang in there, it might not be necessary. Just throwing ideas out there, mmmk?

If you're still short and sitting on a big expensive property, why? Oh, you want to leave it to the kids. Guess what? They'd rather receive a pile of money. Guess what else? They probably don't want it, and dealing with it after you're gone could rupture their relationship with each other forever. Guess what else? Your obligation to them is done. You did a great job, let them fly. I always told my kids I never got anything from anyone, so whatever they get when I'm gone to my glory is a bonus. I gave them a good life, an excellent education, and all they need in life to succeed. Guess what they say? "Damn right, Pop. Go enjoy your life and don't worry about us, we good." Man, I love those kids. Don't tell anyone, but

I plan to help them out when I head to the happy hunting grounds in the sky.

I digress. Back to that house. Can you downsize? Rent? See the chapter on buying/selling properties. How about a renter in your house? silvernet.com finds you fellow senior renters, does the background check, does an eHarmony-type dating service matchup to find someone just like you. They take care of collecting payments, so you don't have to chase anyone around. Senior renters aren't likely to have wild parties or change their Harley oil in your living room. They often help and because they're so closely matched with your own demeanor and interests, they become lifelong friends.

There is also over a trillion dollars in unclaimed retirement fund money out there. Recent legislation funded a new database to find it, which should be up and running soon. In the meantime, reach out to any old employer HR departments, and use the missing money links from Chapter 3.

Where are we at? If it's not close, take some steps back, as I just described. Don't give up hope, get mad, be determined. This book has given you all the tools you need to fix this. If you're in the ballpark, let's proceed and dial things in.

Steps to Prep

After you leave any job, roll your employer-sponsored retirement plans over to your own IRA. This includes 401k, 403b, and 457 plans—but maybe not that last one. Be careful there, as 457 plans are the only one of that group that allows penalty-free withdrawals prior to age 59 1/2. If you're planning FIRE or early retirement, maybe leave it where it is for that reason. Also, some 457 plans for physicians and other highly-compensated individuals have very different rules, so make sure you understand yours.

Otherwise, these plans carry higher fees than you would pay under your own IRA, especially when invested as we describe. You get more investing choices in your own IRA, and more control. Your employer-sponsored plan is free to pick up your account and move it somewhere else, for example, from Fidelity to Great West. I've seen it happen, and received panicked calls from people saying, "I logged in and my money is gone!" Again, the fewer people and rules between you and your money, the better.

If you already have your employer funds invested as we advocate in the chapters on investing, you can often just move the shares themselves over, rather than having to go to cash and reinvest. Employer plans are usually limited, so it's no big deal if you have to do so in retirement plans. Do a trustee-to-trustee electronic direct rollover if possible, rather than an indirect rollover, where you get a paper check to send on to wherever your IRA is. The latter choice is risky—if you don't send that check within sixty days, it will be considered a withdrawal and you risk big penalties and a huge tax bill. The check should be made out to the new brokerage, not you. That's still technically a direct rollover, but, semantics.

If you have target date funds or balanced funds, which comprise both stock and bond funds within your fund, break those out. You want to be positioned in retirement to be able to choose whether to draw from stocks or bonds, depending on which has done better over the year. Having target date or balanced funds takes that power away from you, and could cause you to sell stocks at a loss, which we generally always want to avoid, unless intentionally tax loss harvesting. They're not bad to have in accumulation phase, if the expense ratio is low. Also keep in mind some target date funds will freeze their allocation when the target date is reached, whereas some will continue to change after the target date is reached.

If you have a pension fund, you may have a choice to either take a lump sum or get annual or monthly payments for the rest of your life. This decision has to be made carefully, as there are often many options for things like spousal benefits. In general, I'm a fan of taking that lump sum and investing it as we described. You have full control, and fewer people and rules between you and your money. History is rife with examples of mismanaged pension funds going bust. We've talked about some of those. Who is managing **your** pension money out there, and are they doing it well? In the rare cases where pensions are adjusted for inflation, that becomes a big checkmark in their column, but I'm still skeptical. Good investments are the only thing that's historically been able to stay ahead of inflation.

Risks and Mitigations

The primary risks to retirement are longevity, debt, inflation, and sequence. Let's talk about each one and how to protect yourself from them.

Longevity risk is the risk that you'll live longer than you expected, and can thus run out of money. Some people are so eager to retire they become biased about this and subconsciously assume they'll expire sooner in order to make the numbers work. In planning, I default to age 90, but ask clients if they'd like to adjust that based on their own health, or family history. There are calculators you can use to try to dial it in more, such as longevityillustrator.org and death-clock.org. But hey, we never know when we're going to get hit by a bus or meteorite, amirite?

One way to mitigate longevity risk is to make sure your essential expenses are covered by guaranteed lifetime income sources like Social Security and pensions. The insurance salespeople are yelling, "Annuities!" right now, but I've made my feelings about them known in the chapter on insurances. Bleh. Although I said that sometimes, simple annuities late in life, such as Single Premium Immediate Annuities, aren't as bad. A multi-year guaranteed annuity (MYGA) could help bridge the gap until collecting Social Security. Do the math, consider the risks I talked about in the earlier chapter.

My friends Chris and Jim at my favorite podcast, theretiremen tandirashow.com, call this your Minimum Dignity Floor (MDF), and advocate making sure it's covered by fixed or guaranteed income sources, and use the nest egg for fun money. I'd say that I would consider an ultra-safe withdrawal rate (such as 2%) from a well-invested nest egg to be guaranteed income, but I don't think they do. Different strokes. I'll talk about another solution later in this chapter, for those who are most risk-averse and dig the MDF concept.

Debt risk This is something I rail about throughout the book. But, especially in retirement, you exposure yourself to rising interest rates and the rates on any variable debt such as credit cards, being jacked up beyond your ability to pay. Go into retirement clean, without debt payments, stress, or risk. I can't say it enough! You genuinely feel more free, and isn't that what retirement should feel like? Pay off that mortgage. Now it's your house, and nobody can take it away. The grass feels so much better between your toes! You mitigate debt risk by not having any. Mic drop.

Inflation risk. This is the rising cost of goods and services. Remember the budget you laid out earlier? I bet it was in "today's dollars" and didn't factor in that in ten, twenty, thirty years, those vacations will cost a lot more because of inflation. Your income probably didn't factor inflation either, so that's fine for our current high-level thumbnail view. Remember though, that some income, such as pensions and annuities, don't have COLA adjustments. We'll tell you how to build a precise plan later. You mitigate inflation risk by factoring inflation into your high-fidelity plan, and perhaps in your fixed-income portion of the asset allocation, holding some inflation-protected bond funds.

Tax Bomb. If you find yourself in a situation where most of your money is in pretax/untaxed accounts (401k/403b/457b, traditional IRA) and the math is showing you'll be forced into large RMDs later in life, that's a tax bomb. You don't want to be in the 30+% tax bracket in your mid-70s to the end of your life! The way to mitigate this is strategic Roth conversions and withdrawals in the years you're in lower tax brackets, and perhaps a Qualified Long-Term Annuity Contract (QLAC). A QLAC is a way to carve out a chunk of pretax money in those accounts and set it aside as a deferred annuity that starts later in life (as late as 85!). The result is lower RMDs. You can ladder these and buy inflation protection.

However, the tax man always cometh, and you'll have to pay taxes on the annuity payments when they start. Plus, all the risks and fees I've already presented regarding annuities. If you give to charities, do so as a Qualified Charitable Distribution (QCD) from your pretax IRA after you turn age 70 1/2. It helps with your RMDs, is a simpler way to give (rather than withdrawing, paying taxes, and then giving the post-tax amount), and provides a bigger contribution. One last way to mitigate taxes is to take dividend payments from your brokerage account, as they're qualified long-term dividends and subject to the 0% or 15% long-term capital gains tax bracket. That's not a bad rate!

Sequence risk. This is when the economy and stock market go into decline shortly after your retirement. You're forced to sell shares of your stock when they're devalued, which is never good unless you're intentionally tax-loss harvesting in a brokerage account. Sequence risk is a scare tactic used by insurance salespeople to sell annuities, or for AUM-based advisors to have you give them your money to manage.

Let's go back to our 4% rule example, where you retired with a million dollars, and started taking $40,000, or a safe 4% each year (adjusted up for inflation each year). Assume the stock market tanks 25% during your first year of retirement. If your portfolio was all in stocks (that's silly, but follow along...) your million dollars is now around $750k, and your $40k withdrawal is no longer a safe 4%, it's a possibly unsafe 5.3%. Let's calm down a bit and come back to reality. First, the math around the 4% rule does already factor in market ups and down, so they account for this kind of thing. Second, the 4% rule assumes you're somewhere between 60/40 and 50/50 in your asset allocation. If the market is down, just use your cash and bonds, and don't sell any shares of your stock funds! Jeez.

That's how you mitigate sequence risk. That's why you shouldn't be in target date funds or balanced funds in retirement. In fact, there's a technique called bucketing that mitigates sequence risk. Let's talk about that next.

Bucket Strategies

The bucket strategy for retirees is pretty simple, and simple is good. This technique requires three virtual buckets of money. I say virtual because in reality, your money is spread across different types of accounts in different locations. Let's go back to your retirement budgeting exercise. Subtract your non-nest egg sources of income (Social Security, pension, side hustle, etc) from your first-year monthly expense total.

This is how much cash you'll need per month from your nest egg. Let's call it your **Monthly Nest Egg Cash Need**. Multiply it times twelve for an **Annual Nest Egg Cash Need**. Do that for year two as well, if the expenses aren't the same as year one. The three buckets are as follows. Two years of annual nest egg cash needs in bucket one, sitting in a high-yield FDIC insured savings account. Then, the next 3-5 years of nest egg cash needs in safe US treasury bond funds. The rest in stock. What does this accomplish? You're now protected from "sequence risk" for a down stock market for up to seven years (which is pretty unheard in recent times)! You don't have to sell any stocks while they're down.

It's important to juxtapose these buckets against your asset allocation. As you can imagine, if you've got significant assets, setting your buckets up this way could result in a big overbalance toward stocks. It could be well outside your natural level of risk tolerance and cause lots of stress when the market is down. If you don't have a big nest egg, the opposite can happen. If your asset allocation is

40/60 after creating your buckets, you could run out of money. I would start with your desired asset allocation, somewhere between 60/40 and 50/50 going into retirement. Do a little math. Does that 40% or 50% fixed income cover at lasts 5-7 years of cash needs per our calculations? If so, make sure two years worth is in cash and you're good to go (even if it's much more than 5-7 years worth). If you have a higher risk tolerance, this is a way of giving yourself permission to have an asset allocation more tilted toward stocks, as long as the math still works.

At the start of year one of retirement, you simply either transfer the needed cash for that year over to checking/savings, or you can set it up as an automatic monthly payment, just like a paycheck. I like the latter approach. You might be wondering what happens at the end-of-year one. Your cash bucket is now down to only one year! Here's what you do. Assess how your stocks and bonds did over the past year. If the stocks were up, but bonds were down, go ahead and take some of those stock winnings off the table by selling a year's worth of nest egg cash needs and transferring it to your cash bucket. If the stocks were down but the bonds were up, as usually happens, do so with the bonds funds.

This also has the desired effect of rebalancing your portfolio back to where it should be! If neither sector did well, as happens infrequently in history (but did in 2022!), you can just sit pat. That's why you have two years of nest egg cash needs in cash. Another approach is to just let your dividends and interest payments go to cash throughout the year, instead of reinvesting them, and using that money to refill your buckets.

To get back to the Minimum Dignity Floor concept, you could just use a high-fidelity planner (as discussed below) to calculate your annual nest egg cash needs for the rest of your life, and put that into something like a bond and/or CD ladder (as discussed in

Chapter 10). That saves the annual exercise of filling the buckets, but you still have to rebalance annually if your asset allocation is out of whack. You could also put money in a 30-year US treasury bond if interest rates are good, and live off those interest payments (these are not callable bonds). If you do things that way, your essential/non-discretionary costs for food, transportation, health care, shelter are covered. This also means the remaining money is all "fun money!" You can spend as much as you want each year, but when it's gone, it's gone (and hence, so is the fun?).

High-Fidelity Planning

What we covered so far are some high-level ways to map out your FIRE or traditional retirement. I wouldn't pull the trigger on such a huge financial decision based on just those exercises. The retirement picture is a complex puzzle of inter-related pieces, such as taxes, health care, investment decisions, pensions, Social Security, inflation, market performance, and so on. You really need something to pull all that together for you, because changes in one area affect all the others. You can't do this by going to a Social Security calculator, a separate tax calculator, safe withdrawal rate calculator, etc. Every piece affects the other.

There are many choices out there. Personal finance tools like Quicken and Personal Capital (now called Empower) have retirement planners built in. Some are more detailed, or high fidelity, others are not. Many of the tools intentionally, out of necessity, dumb things down because most people don't have the knowledge that you do right now after reading this book. That hurts you since you can plan in more detail! New Retirement (newretirement.com) is pretty good. The free version is dumbed down, but the paid version isn't bad for people with a better-than-average knowledge of finances and retirement concepts. For FIRE advocates, Lauren Boland maintains the Crowdsourced Financial Independence and Retire Early Simulator (cFIRESim) tool at cfiresim.com and there are some great new features coming. It even has a tutorial!

As a registered, professional investment advisor and financial planner, I've tried some of the pro-only power tools. These are truly high fidelity, but typically hard to use, very expensive, and not available to regular consumers. My whole deal is advocating for people to take control of their own financial lives, so it would be hypocrisy for me to use one of those.

So, what do I use? My go-to tool is the Pralana Gold Retirement Calculator (PRC) pralanaretirementcalculator.com. It's dirt-cheap and on par or better with those very expensive pro tools the planners use. It's high-fidelity—that's good, but it means you need the foundational knowledge we've covered in order to use it well. In its current form, PRC runs on Microsoft Excel. That's a big advantage for privacy-focused folks, because your data stays on your computer (and hopefully you back it up). After this current year (2023) it will be available as a web-based tool, but it will still allow you to keep your data local. I receive no compensation of any form for recommending this tool. I love it because it's amazing. The owner/developer is a former engineer and has an altruistic mindset, just like I do.

PRC will take your current financial situation, ask you for some projections about the future in terms of inflation and market performance (you can use the defaults), and then take your goals for future expenses. It has tools to optimize your Social Security (I still recommend using the Open Social Security tool and plugging those numbers into PRC), things like Roth conversions, asset location withdrawal optimization (what accounts and how much to withdraw each year for tax and performance optimization), and so much more. It has a fantastic PDF user manual (gasp!) and a very robust discussion forum on the website. Even a Facebook group that I run!

The graphs and reports will give you a clear picture and roadmap of your personal finances throughout the rest of your life. The primary thing PRC does is to run hundreds of Monte Carlo random simulations and past historical trends and then tell you what your odds of succeeding are, for both your essential and discretionary spending. We typically shoot for 90% chance of success or better, since you do have the ability to adapt and adjust as you go, now that you're in full control, have a clear roadmap and all this knowledge. We want the essential expenses to be at 100%. The most valuable features in PRC are also the When Can I Retire calculator and the How Much More Can I spend calculator (expense smoothing). It's telling you how to have your best retirement, without worry!

Your retirement/financial plan should also be a living document. Tax laws change, retirement laws change, actuarial tables for things like Social Security, inherited IRAs, and so forth, always change. *You* always change! Your future self may not have the same goals as your younger self. Many financial planners will charge you for your plan, then hand you a two-inch thick binder (that most people never read) and say sayonara, or, "Now, let's get to the part where you hand over your money for me to manage and enrich myself..." Your financial/retirement plan should be a living document. No matter what tool you use, update it each year as part of your annual financial housekeeping checklist. PRC comes out with a new version each year around mid-January, and I often refresh these plans with my clients, or urge them to do so on their own and review the results with me. You can see a rough example of what one of my plans looks like at emancipare.com/sample.

Reverse Mortgages/HELOC

A final note on a tool that's often pitched to retirees—reverse mortgages. It's really upsetting to see actors who played trusted figures on television shows and movies now hawking products that could be so disastrous for seniors. Commercials for reverse mortgages are ubiquitous. These loans are only for those age 62 or older. In a reverse mortgage, you get cash based on the value of your home, and you don't have to pay it back immediately. Any time you hear you don't have to pay something back immediately, sirens should go off in your head, along with a flashing sign that says "interest is accruing, the debt is growing!"

You can get that cash in a lump sum, as monthly payments, in a line of credit, or some combination of those choices. You can only do this once. The reverse mortgage must typically be paid when you move out of the home, sell the home, or the last person on the deed passes away. You may not plan to move, but often life happens. The home may become a problem because of illness or injury as we get older. You may desire to be closer to your grandkids, or you may later get the bug for warmer weather. Having that reverse mortgage looming would be an impediment to your plans.

Here are a few other reasons a reverse mortgage can be a bad idea.

1. Equity: As in the cash-out refinance discussed above, you are essentially borrowing on the equity of your home. So it's bad for many of the same reasons listed for that option.

2. Fees: Any mortgage involves closing costs, and this is

no exception. See the fees listed in cash-out refinancing above.

3. Government Benefits: A reverse mortgage can affect your eligibility for things like Social Security Supplemental Security Income (SSI) and Medicaid.

4. Shady Operators: This space is filled with predators who are anxious to take advantage of senior citizens. In recent years, the rules were tightened up to make this less of a scam, but nonetheless, it remains a very poor choice in almost all circumstances.

5. Legacy: If you want to leave your home to your heirs, this complicates the picture. They would have to pay off the reverse mortgage.

Borrowing on your equity also leaves less for them to inherit. If you feel you must go this route, contact me for a review of your complete financial picture and analysis for better alternatives. Ensure that your loan is insured by the Federal Housing Administration under the Home Equity Conversion Mortgage (HECM) program.

Some pre-retirees will also take out a home equity line of credit (HELOC) while they're still working. It acts like an "in case of emergency break glass" safety valve. If your personal finance temperament is such that you've always used credit cards to buy things you can't afford to pay cash on, this "tool" could be disastrous. Same with cash-out refinancing. Keep your retirement simple and stress-free. Stay out of debt. If you've done a good, precise plan, this should never be necessary. I've given you too many other, better ways to mitigate any unexpected problems throughout this book!

CHAPTER FIFTEEN

Bye Now! Go Forth and Prosper!

YOU. CAN. DO. THIS!

"Everything bad that happened, happened for a reason ... to teach us not to do it again."

Tommy Iommi

I really hope people read this book, and I hope it changes some lives. It's not a profit motive, it's just what makes me happy. Remember that superhero story from the beginning of this book? Hopefully, at least my kids and grandkids read it, and abide by it long after I'm gone. Perhaps I'll be able to buy a used RV, or maybe just the steering wheel as a start. That whole living in a van down by the river thing always sounded good to me. As a frustrated and failed writer of fiction, I know all about rejection and hurtful reviews. I'm a lifelong writer—it's in my DNA. I finish this book as I always do, with similar visions as Ralphie in the movie A Christmas Story, receiving A++++ reviews and being carried out of the classroom on the shoulders of my teacher and classmates. I'm prepared for a similar fate to Ralphie, but if I know I've changed at least one life, I'm happy. How many of us get to do that in life? If this book helped you, please take a minute to write a review. I read them. If you took issue, didn't like it, or found an error, just send me an email at bill@emancipare.com instead. I'd appreciate it. A lot of time went into this project. It's also a living document.

As I wrap this project up, we're just getting back from an impromptu, unplanned three-day trip to the beach in early April. We dropped everything and just went, despite a tight deadline to complete this book. Hey, it's not mid-80s in April very often in our neck of the woods! The ability to do so is what this book and financial freedom are all about. I'm my own boss. It was my deadline for the book. I told myself to go ahead, you only live once, Bill. I'm back refreshed, recharged, a little sunburnt (for the love of God, please don't tell my mom). and *so* excited to finish this project and get it into your hands.

But, a trip to the beach and boardwalk is quite telling. I stood behind parents who angrily told their kids they couldn't play another game or go on another ride because, "We can't afford it." (I'm a stealthy slipper of large bills into open purses in cases such as this.) I also saw countless people of all ages who had taken those early April weekdays off to join me on the beach for the sunrise. They were clearly happy and relaxed. They had done something right, and that's the kind of life I want for you. Imagine what a happier place this world would be if we all had that luxury!

Make sure to read the appendices in this book. Maybe print them out and post them up somewhere front-and-center as a reminder. Especially those best and worst practices, and personal finance checklists. Do me a favor—each time you gawk at a new car, or even get ready to pull out your credit card for some impulse purchase, take a beat and ask yourself if it's worth more time at the beach, leaving the workforce earlier, more time with grandkids, or maybe that someday (and sooner) lake house or beach house.

There's a trap to building wealth. If you're like me, you grew up knowing what it's like to not be able to have everything you want. Actually, so did my kids. Even when we could afford some things they wanted (the newest phones, a new car) we didn't give it to them. We wanted them to be humble, to learn what it's like to make good financial decisions and work for things. We always made sure they saved and had some skin in the game. When they reached driving age, they had to work and pay their own insurance for the privilege.

Suppose you build wealth and set things up so your kids never have to struggle financially. Maybe you leave them a great inheritance when they're young. But, what's that going to do to their kids, who may then never know what it's like to be like normal people, and have to sometimes do without, to have to save up, and scrape by? We've seen countless examples of these types of folks in our society—the trust fund babies who never really had to work, always had the best of everything, the silver spoon set. You probably knew some of them from school. Were they good people? They often aren't. Often the ones we see in the news or social media come off as entitled jerks, never having enough, no compassion or empathy for others, not understanding they had the road paved for them. They're in a competition with their peers to always want more, more, more, to the detriment of the rest of us. They've paid to get the system rigged so they don't pay taxes, and laugh at us for doing so.

My point is this—keep your kids and grandkids humble. Sure, we love them and want to spoil them. But understand when you are actually doing harm. Teach your children. It's the best gift you can give and will endure long after you stop handing out cash and gifts. They'll remember you well and look back fondly at your lessons and hopefully pass them on as generational knowledge.

The other thing I'd like to ask is that you be generous. After you've done the hard work and "made it," it's easy to then look down on anyone that needs help and say, "Heck, I did it, so can they." Many of these people fight generational poverty, have endured traumatic abuse, have mental or health issues, and other factors that the rest of us don't know about that make it almost impossible for them to follow in our footsteps. Tell people about this book. Give out copies. Share your new knowledge. Above all, be generous and kind! It really is an important ingredient in the recipe of happiness and self-esteem. Pay it forward. Your kids are watching.

We're often groomed to see the gold standard of success in life as being wealthy, having "made it." There's nothing wrong with that, but as I've shown, it's not really that hard to do! I talked about being a unicorn earlier in the book, but in terms of a financial unicorn. If you want to be something better, be a *life* unicorn—one of those few people these days that genuinely care about others, take a little time each day to do something nice for a perfect stranger that may need a little help. Pick up the tab for an overwhelmed parent in line at the fast food joint. Give to your favorite causes each month, on autopilot. Organizations like the ASPCA, Sierra Club, National Pediatric Cancer Foundation, and so many others always need the help. You'll feel better about yourself. You'll make a difference in this world.

Aside from the ways you can help people with your newfound wealth, you can enhance your happiness simply by building up your self-image. Smile at that person wearing a scowl, find something to compliment them about. They've probably endured a lifetime of getting messed over. Let that stressed out mom merge in on the highway, let them into your lane even if it feels they're cutting you off. Pick up your trash, and pick up other people's.

I'd like to end with this homework assignment (you didn't think you were getting off that easy, did you?) This exercise involves George Kinder's (kinderinstitute.com) three life questions. It's useful to think through these, and although morbid, can put things into perspective. They are:

1. Imagine that you are financially secure and that you have all the money you need for the rest of your life. How would you live your life? Would you change anything? What would you do? Let yourself go. Don't hold back your dreams. Will you change your life and how will you do it?

2. This time, you visit your doctor, who tells you that you have five to ten years left to live. The good part is that you won't ever feel sick. The bad news is that you will have no notice of the moment of your death. What will you do in the time you have remaining? Will you change your life, and how will you do it?

3. This time, your doctor shocks you with the news that you have only one day left to live. Notice what feelings arise as you confront your very real mortality. Reflecting on your life, on all your accomplishments, as well as on all the things that will remain undone, ask yourself: What did I

miss? Who did I not get to be? What did I not get to do?

Think through that, along with your partner/spouse, if you have one. It should motivate you even more to follow the principles and techniques laid out in this book. As the title of this final chapter says, go forth and prosper! I genuinely wish you all the happiness you deserve.

The End

"When we give cheerfully and accept gratefully, everyone is blessed."

Maya Angelou

"No one has ever become poor by giving."

Anne Frank

Appendix A: Power Tools

I've mentioned a bunch of tools throughout this book, but wanted to provide a comprehensive list for you.

Consumer Financial Protection Bureau (CFPB) consumerfinance.gov This is an **absolute gold mine** of **free** personal finance resources. Yes, **free, free, free**, even the beautiful full-color **printed** materials that ship right to your home. It's a shame that so many people don't know about and aren't taking advantage of these great tools.

Pralana Gold Retirement Calculator pralanaretirementcalculator.com This is my go-to planning tool, an inexpensive high-fidelity financial/retirement calculator that's available for consumers. I discuss it in Chapter 14.

The Retirement and IRA Show Podcast theretirementandirashow.com Chris and Jim are the go-to for in-depth advice and analysis of all things personal finance, financial planning, Social Security, and so much more. Their banter is entertaining!

The Simple Path to Wealth This is a wonderful book by JL Collins. It's concise, entertaining, readable, and out of the wall-sized bookshelf of books in my office on personal finance topics, it's my favorite!

Investopedia investopedia.com is my go-to source for clean objective financial information and fact-checking. Subscribe to their daily email.

Ed Slott/IRA Help irahelp.com Ed is the most respected authority in the field when it comes to IRAs, taxes, and all things retirement personal finance.

Can I Retire Yet blog caniretireyet.com Darrow Kirkpatrick and Chris Mamula post regular content on FIRE and other retirement considerations.

Optimal Finance Daily podcast This every-day ten minute slice of great personal finance life will give you so much knowledge! Tell me you don't have ten minutes a day while watching the dog poop, exercising, or commuting?

Early Retirement Now earlyretirementnow.com Karsten, or Big ERN as he's known, provides a wonderful blog and set of tools. One is a safe withdrawal rate (SWR) calculator, which you can use to figure out what your own personal safe withdrawal rate is. The 4% rule is based on 30 years. Maybe you're a FIRE person and need a SWR for 40 or 50 years.

Vertex42 Calculators vertex42.com Excel and Google Sheets based financial calculators for free and on the cheap. Use the debt reduction calculator as a guide to slaying your debt and seeing how much money you'll save, as well as the payoff dates! Also see calculator.net and bankrate.com for good calculators.

Open Social Security Calculator opensocialsecurity.com This is a great, high-fidelity Social Security optimizer/calculator. Don't forget to check the little box at the top to get the advanced inputs, and play with the tools toward the bottom to explore strategies and what-if scenarios. The owner, Mike Piper, also has a great book on Social Security.

cFIRESim cfiresim.com is a crowdsourced FIRE calculator/simulator. Very fun to play with, and free!

Emancipare Sample Financial Plan emancipare.com/sample Use this as a guide to the types of things you should be paying attention to in planning your financial/retirement roadmap. See the blog on my website as well for my takes on different personal finance matters.

Budgets Are Sexy blog budgetsaresexy.com J. Money is a Mohawk-styled personal finance/FIRE blogger who provides funny and useful content on side hustles and other topics.

BogleHeads bogleheads.org This is my go-to web site and discussion forum for all questions related to investing and personal finance. It's populated by very smart people who are very responsive and opinionated. They're disciples of the late, great Jack Bogle and also called Vanguardians. The site also features great articles, books for sale, and tools.

Portfolio Visualizer portfoliovisualizer.com This great site allows you to compare portfolios side-by-side. Does your advisor claim they're paying for themselves by investing you such that you're beating the market over the long haul? Here's where you can find out for sure (don't forget to include asset management and all other fees!)

Appendix B:
Best/Worst Practices

These are thumbnail lists of the best and worst financial practices. Before people go nuts, please affix the caveat "in most cases." There are sometimes very slim use cases where some of the worst practices might be necessary. For example, your house is about to be repossessed and you have no other option. Read this book so you know the proper application!

Financial Best Practices

- Know your monthly cash flow and expenses

- Disavow debt

- Have a monthly financial meeting recap/plan with your significant other or just yourself

- Do an annual update of your financial roadmap

- Rebalance your investments annually

- Save and invest—buy low and sell high

- Freeze your credit at TransUnion, Experian, Equifax

- Keep your mortgage or rent cost below 25% of your *take-home* income

- Never, ever click on links in emails or texts—open a browser and go to the site directly

- Make sure your wills, insurances, and beneficiaries are set up correctly

Financial Worst Practices (In Almost All Cases)

- Whole Life Insurance (cash value, universal, indexed/IUL, maximum premium indexed/MPI, variable)

- Annuities (other than very strategic SPIAs or MYGAs)

- Cash-Out Refinancing

- Reverse Mortgages

- Bankruptcy

- Panic selling your investments when the market drops

- Borrowing money from your retirement plans

- Buying long-term care coverage inside a whole life insurance policy

- Paying asset management fees, high expense ratios, loads/commissions

The Most Important Questions You Should _Always_ Ask

- Are there any discounts for veterans, health care workers, teachers, AAA, AARP, employees of xx, members of xx...

- Can you do any better than that?

- Do I want this more than my freedom?

Appendix C: Emancipare Yearly Financial Calendar

Below is a monthly calendar of the topics we cover with our year-round clients. It's a good guide to the topics you should be addressing, and when!

January Retirement plan refresh, start of year checklist, goals review, milestones calendar, autopilot update.

February Insurances review, yearly vacation/travel saving strategy.

March College/trade/tech school planning.

April Review taxes prior to filing. File on time!

May Review beneficiaries/will/trust/estate plan, document organization.

June Pull and review credit reports, ID theft protections.

July Mid-year checkup/plan update, cash flow check.

August Accountability, open topics, pick-a-class (below).

September Career planning/small business discussion.

October Review employer open enrollment choices. File the FAFSA early!

November Holiday season prep, Accountability, open topics, pick-a-class (below).

December Rebalancing/replenishing assets/buckets, year-end tax moves/strategy, charitable giving/gifting, RMD check.

Classes/Learning Topics

- Investing Basics

- Advanced Investing/Taxes

- Pralana Retirement Calculator

- Buying/Selling Property

- Buying/Selling Vehicles

- Cash Flow/Budgeting

- Side Hustles/Small Businesses

- (Not) Paying for College, Tech, Trade School

- Smart Consumer: Save on Everything

- All About Insurances

- Social Security/Medicare Basics

- Retirement Planning

About the Author

Bill Hines is an AFCPE® Accredited Financial Counselor®, Ramsey Master Financial Coach, Investment Advisor Representative, and Financial/Retirement/FIRE planner located in the Lehigh Valley region of Pennsylvania.

He is the founder of Money Coach Group, Inc (an organization that has helped countless clients emerge from debt to a better life) and Emancipare (an organization that provides honest, ethical, inexpensive, flat-fee, fee-only, fiduciary investment advice and financial planning). A proud United States Air Force Veteran, he used his GI Bill benefits for a Bachelor of Science degree from New York Institute of Technology and an Associate Degree in Information Technology from Tulsa Jr College.

Originally hailing from the Garden State of New Jersey, Bill has also lived for many years in Hershey, PA (Chocolatetown, USA). He has dedicated his professional life to helping people rise up from money stress, become financially independent, invest well, avoid getting scammed and ripped off, and living their one life on their own terms, each and every day.

You can reach and follow Bill at bill@emancipare.com, emanci pare.com, @EmancipareFIRE (Twitter & Facebook)

Also By Bill Hines

Show and Sell 2023: Selling Your Home Today, A Cautionary Tale (available at Amazon, Barnes & Noble, and other booksellers as eBook, audiobook, and paperback)

Upcoming (January 2024): Planning Your Financial Life with Pralana

Recommended Fiction from Wild Lake Press

Farawayer (literary fiction), "...a sweeping literary travelogue that evokes Kerouac's On the Road and Salinger's Catcher in the Rye..." Hitchhiking and motorcycling are a means to a destination, but you can't outrun your demons.

Vigilante Angels Trilogy (noir crime), If you were going to die, who would you kill? A dark, gritty trilogy. Buckle up and prepare to ride a roller-coaster of fear, anger, vengeance, and vigilante justice.

DroidMesh Trilogy (all-ages sci-fi, teen hero with disabilities), Can the sorrow of a father, the challenge of a feat never accomplished, and the promise of normalcy for a son who has never known it motivate a man beyond his ethical boundaries? What happens when it all goes wrong?

Acknowledgments

I'd like to thank the following people for pitching in and doing an advance copy/beta read. Their comments, advice, and catches have been a big help in getting this right.

Matthew Giovanelli (PizzaMan)—One of those DIY personal finance afficionados who are so knowledgeable and curious they could be in the profession. He holds court on the Pralana Retirement Calculator forum, sharing his curiosity, knowledge, and wisdom.

Lindsey Slattery AFC®—Lindsey provided the type of diligent, thorough review that one would expect from an AFC®, and more! Thank you for the many helpful comments and edits. You have a book in you as well, I know it and I'll return the favor!

Lori Hines, Derek Hines, Frank McGhee, for their additional comments and catches.

Made in the USA
Middletown, DE
29 September 2023

39762243R00156